THE
BOOK LOVERS' MISCELLANY

THE
BOOK LOVERS'
MISCELLANY

Claire Cock-Starkey

Bodleian Library
UNIVERSITY OF OXFORD

First published in 2017 by the Bodleian Library
Broad Street, Oxford OX1 3BG
www.bodleianshop.co.uk

ISBN 978 1 85124 471 3

The publisher would like to thank Francesca Galligan
and Stephen Hebron for their help with this book.

Cover design by Dot Little at the Bodleian Library
Designed and typeset in 11 on 13 Perpetua
by illuminati, Grosmont
Printed and bound in Croatia by Zrinski D.D.
on 100 gsm Munken Premium cream

British Library Catalogue in Publishing Data
A CIP record of this publication is available from the British Library

INTRODUCTION

> Books are the quietest and most constant of
> friends; they are the most accessible and wisest
> of counselors, and the most patient of teachers.

> —*Charles William Eliot*

The book, in its many guises, has been around for
many thousands of years, educating, inspiring and
entertaining us. From the earliest religious works,
minutely decorated and crafted by hand, to modern
ephemeral paperbacks and self-published e-books,
books have maintained a vital cultural role. Ever since
the first scrolls and manuscripts we have had an urge to
collect and share books in their many forms, protect-
ing our cultural heritage and ensuring the survival of
many of our most precious works.

A book is not simply an object of beauty in itself;
treasures can also be found between its covers. Books
are full of possibilities – transporting readers to

far-flung places, back or forwards in time, allowing us to walk in another's shoes and gain fresh perspectives. So any celebration of books must also consider writers and writing. Thus George Orwell's writing tips, literary movements of note, Poets Laureate, recurring characters, novels with invented languages and notable book prizes are just some of the themes included here.

Books are not just about their literary merit but also embody a whole technological history from papyrus scrolls through handmade codices to modern mass-produced novels. *The Book Lovers' Miscellany* represents a virtual museum of the book; each aspect of the development of the book, from inks to bindings, is here explored.

Never one to shy away from creating a list, I have collected and curated many here, including the oldest known books, the most translated books, best-selling children's books, alternative book titles, movies which started life as books, pen names, odd book titles and unfinished novels. I have endeavoured to translate my love of books into readable snippets to amuse and amaze (and perhaps win you a few points in the pub quiz too).

Inevitably any book about books could go on indefinitely, covering ever more obscure facts and falling down many literary rabbit holes. But I hope that I have created a celebration of books, writers and writing, a joyful, quirky and fascinating compendium of bookish delights to interest fledgling collectors and confirmed bibliophiles alike.

Claire Cock-Starkey

NOMS DE PLUME

A nom de plume is a pen name or alias, which for various reasons an author might decide to use when their book is published. The Brontë sisters originally published their works under male names to disguise their sex; J.K. Rowling used the nom de plume Robert Galbraith to publish a book in a completely different genre (a trick used by a number of authors, including Stephen King and Ruth Rendell); and Charles Lutwidge Dodgson (Lewis Carroll) created his pen name to keep his academic career separate from his writing career. Some notable noms de plume are:

REAL NAME	NOM DE PLUME
Samuel Langhorne Clemens[*]	Mark Twain
Charles Lutwidge Dodgson	Lewis Carroll
Stephen King	Richard Bachman

---

[*] There are a number of stories for the origin of Samuel Clemens's pen name. One suggests it came about from his former profession piloting a steamboat on the Mississippi River. When testing the depth of the water to see if it was deep enough for a steamboat to pass through, the crew would shout 'mark twain', twain meaning 'two' and signifying there was only a shallow 2 fathoms of water, which was the minimum depth for a boat to pass through. Another story recounts that the nickname derived from Clemens's love of a good drink and lack of money to pay for that drink. It was said that he often frequented the Old Saloon Bar in Virginia City, which marked a patron's tab in chalk on the wall. Clemens would so frequently ask them to 'mark twain' (chalk up two drinks) that it became a nickname. Clemens himself spun what is thought to have been another tall tale of the name's origins, claiming that he took it from an old pen name of Captain Isaiah Sellers, who wrote the river news under that sobriquet but who died in 1863 and so had no further use of it. Whichever story is the real one we shall probably never know.

Anton Chekhov[*]	Man Without a Spleen
Mary Ann Evans	George Eliot
François-Marie Arouet	Voltaire
Charlotte Brontë	Currer Bell
Emily Brontë	Ellis Bell
Anne Brontë	Acton Bell
Margaret Astrid Lindholm Ogden	Robin Hobb
Ricardo Eliécer Neftalí Reyes Basoalto	Pablo Neruda
Steven Billy Mitchell	Andy McNab
Ruth Rendell	Barbara Vine
C.S. Lewis	Clive Hamilton
Eric Arthur Blair	George Orwell
David John Moore Cornwell	John le Carré
Joanne (J.K.) Rowling	Robert Galbraith
Agatha Christie	Mary Westmacott
Nicci Gerard & Sean French	Nicci French
Cecil Day-Lewis	Nicholas Blake
William Sydney Porter	O. Henry
Kingsley Amis	Robert Markham

---

[*] Russian playwright Anton Chekhov used numerous pseudonyms over the course of his career, generally with an absurd twist – such as: Nut #6, My Brother's Brother, The Prosaic Poet and – most frequently, in an allusion to his medical training – Man Without a Spleen.

TRILOGIES, TETRALOGIES, PENTALOGIES AND SO ON

A group of three books by the same author telling an ongoing story with the same characters or exploring the same themes is known as a trilogy and has been a popular and successful device for authors to continue developing a story. However, in recent years the number of volumes in a series has grown, most notably to seven in the case of the Harry Potter novels by J.K. Rowling, leading to the need for a new term to cover these longer series.

The words used to describe various series of books, and some notable examples, are:

TWO BOOKS – *dilogy or duology**
Robert Graves, *I, Claudius* and *Claudius the God*

THREE BOOKS – *trilogy†*
Philip Pullman, *His Dark Materials* trilogy
Roddy Doyle, Barrytown trilogy
Mervyn Peake, *Gormenghast‡* trilogy
Paul Auster, *The New York Trilogy*
Stieg Larsson, Millennium trilogy

---

* This definition is debated, as there is no agreement on the correct term. Some use *diptych*, although strictly speaking this should only apply to one story spread across two books.

† Perhaps one of the most famous trilogies, J R R. Tolkien's *The Lord of the Rings*, is not a trilogy at all. Tolkien saw the story as one work and it was only split into three because of post-war paper shortages.

‡ Originally conceived as an ongoing series, the books were stopped at three by Peake's death, and thus form an unintentional trilogy.

FOUR BOOKS – *tetralogy or quartet*
Stephanie Meyer, *Twilight* tetralogy
Yukio Mishima, *The Sea of Fertility* tetralogy
John Updike, Rabbit Angstrom tetralogy
Lawrence Durrell, *The Alexandria Quartet*

FIVE BOOKS – *pentalogy or quintet*
James Dashner, *The Maze Runner* series
Lynne Reid Banks, *The Indian in the Cupboard* series
Douglas Adams, *The Hitchhiker's Guide to the Galaxy* series[*]

SIX BOOKS – *hexalogy or sextet*
Olivia Manning, *Fortunes of War* hexalogy
Frank Herbert, *Dune* hexalogy
Anthony Trollope, *The Chronicles of Barsetshire*

SEVEN BOOKS – *heptalogy*
J.K. Rowling, Harry Potter heptalogy
C.S. Lewis, *The Chronicles of Narnia*
Marcel Proust, *À la recherche du temps perdu*
Gore Vidal, *Narratives of Empire* heptalogy

---

[*] Adams liked to refer to his work as 'a trilogy in five parts'.

PAPYRUS

The papyrus plant (*Cyperus papyrus*) grows all across the Nile valley and was used by the Ancient Egyptians since *c.* 3000 BC to create a paper-like material to write on. To make papyrus strips of pith from the stalks of the papyrus plant are laid side by side and then another layer is added on top at right angles; this is then weighted down and dried. In Roman times the use of papyrus spread to Europe, and papal bulls continued to be transcribed onto papyrus until 1022. However, papyrus tended to degrade in the European climate and so vellum (*see page 23*) or parchment was more frequently used until papermaking techniques were imported into Europe from China in the eleventh century.

A number of ancient scrolls on papyrus survive from Egypt, including the *Book of the Dead*.* In the late eighteenth century a whole library of charred papyrus scrolls was unearthed in Herculaneum near Naples that had been buried by the eruption of Mount Vesuvius in

---

* The Book of the Dead was the name given in the nineteenth century to copies of an ancient Egyptian book of spells entitled *Spells for Going Forth by Day*, which gave instructions on how to navigate the afterlife. Only the rich and powerful might own a copy of the text as each one was handwritten by a scribe and personalized. The papyrus scrolls would be rolled up and placed inside a statue or tucked beside the mummified body and sealed in the tomb. One of the oldest most complete Books of the Dead to have been found dates from *c.* 950 BC and was made for Nestanebisheru, the daughter of a high priest. The beautifully illustrated papyrus scroll was originally 37 metres long, but was divided into ninety-six separate panels so that it could be studied and preserved at its home at the British Museum.

79 AD – these damaged scrolls were gifted to Napoleon by the King of Naples and now reside in the library of the Institut de France in Paris, where scientists are working to scan and decipher their contents.

UNESCO WORLD BOOK CAPITALS

Since 2001 UNESCO has selected a city to become World Book Capital for the term of one year, running from one World Book and Copyright Day on 23 April (*see page 28*) to the next. To choose a book capital, UNESCO consults with the International Publishers Association, the International Federation of Library Associations and the International Booksellers Federation to select a city which is hosting a significant programme of events to encourage and promote books and reading in the upcoming year. Since its inception in 2001 the World Book Capitals have been:

2001 Madrid, Spain | 2002 Alexandria, Egypt
2003 New Delhi, India | 2004 Antwerp, Belgium
2005 Montreal, Canada | 2006 Turin, Italy
2007 Bogota, Columbia | 2008 Amsterdam,
Netherlands | 2009 Beirut, Lebanon | 2010
Ljubljana, Slovenia | 2011 Buenos Aires, Argentina
2012 Yerevan, Armenia | 2013 Bangkok, Thailand
2014 Port Harcourt, Nigeria | 2015 Incheon,
South Korea | 2016 Wrocław, Poland
2017 Conakry, Republic of Guinea

BANNED BOOKS

Over the years many books have been suppressed due to obscenity, libel, heresy* or the inclusion of state secrets. The act of censorship itself can be very revealing of the changing attitudes and morals of society. Below are ten notable works which have faced bans.

Spycatcher by PETER WRIGHT   Former MI5 intelligence officer Peter Wright attempted to publish his autobiographical work *Spycatcher* in 1985 but was thwarted by the British government, which secured an injunction to prevent the book being published in Britain on grounds of a threat to national security. However, despite ongoing legal battles the book was published in both Scotland and Australia; by 1988 the law lords ruled that the book could be published in Great Britain as any secrets were already spilled. Naturally the controversy meant the book was a huge international bestseller.

Lady Chatterley's Lover by D.H. LAWRENCE   *Lady Chatterley's Lover* was banned in Britain from its publication in 1928 until it came to trial in 1960: one of the most famous obscenity cases ever heard in Britain. The book tells the story of the adulterous relationship

---

* From *c.* 1559 to 1966 the Roman Catholic Church maintained the *Index Librorum Prohibitorum,* an index of books it deemed immoral or heretical. The index recommended either the banning of entire works or the expunging of certain passages. Hundreds of books were listed on the index over the years, including: John Locke's *An Essay Concerning Human Understanding* (1689); Voltaire's *Candide* (1759); Edward Gibbon's *The History of the Decline and Fall of the Roman Empire* (1776–89); and the complete works of Émile Zola.

between an upper-class woman and a working-class man and uses explicit imagery and sexual language, which at that time was unusual and shocking. Challenged under a new obscenity law, its publisher Penguin was acquitted when it was proved that the book had sufficient 'literary merit'.

Wild Swans by JUNG CHANG An account of 100 years of Chinese history through the eyes of Chang's grandmother, mother and herself, *Wild Swans* is one of the most successful non-fiction books of all time, selling over 10 million copies and being translated into thirty-seven different languages. The book provides an unflinchingly honest account of life under the rule of Mao. For this reason the book and all Chang's subsequent works have been banned from publication in China ever since.

All Quiet on the Western Front by ERICH MARIA RE-MARQUE A German novel first serialized in 1928 about the horrors of trench warfare during the First World War, *All Quiet on the Western Front* has come to be seen as a great anti-war work, highlighting the futility of conflict. At the time of publication the book struck a chord with many who had lived through the war and it went on to be made into a very successful Hollywood film. However, as the Nazi party rose to power many began to criticize the book for denigrating the German war effort and accused Remarque of exaggerating the atrocities of war in order to promote his pacifist agenda. The Nazis felt the book was completely at odds with their ideology and the image they wished to present of the perfect German soldier, so the book was publicly burnt and banned from sale.

Doctor Zhivago by Boris Pasternak This romantic masterpiece was published in 1958 but immediately suppressed by the Stalinist government, which accused Pasternak of romanticizing pre-Revolution life in Russia and maligning the peasants' struggle. The book was smuggled out of Russia in parts and translated and published around the world to great critical acclaim, earning Pasternak the Nobel Prize for Literature in 1958. The book's success did little for Pasternak, who was banned from collecting the award and ejected from the Soviet Writers' Union, effectively ending his writing career. Pasternak died in 1960, not living to see the 1965 film version of his book with Omar Sharif as the eponymous character. In 1987 as part of Mikhail Gorbachev's reforms *Doctor Zhivago* was finally published in Russia.

1984 by George Orwell This dystopian novel was first published in 1949 and Orwell's terrifying vision of a totalitarian regime has raised ire ever since. It was banned in Russia under Stalin for its negative portrayal of Communism and has been challenged (complained about or confiscated) repeatedly in American schools and libraries over its overtly political message, making it one of the American Library Association's top five most challenged books of all time.

Ulysses by JAMES JOYCE   This modernist novel, which tells the story of a day in the life of Dubliner Leopold Bloom, was first serialized in 1918 and then published as a whole in Paris in 1922, having already caught the eye of the censors. Its challenging style, using a stream-of-consciousness narrative and covering the very smallest details of Bloom's life (including some very intimate moments) was groundbreaking, and yet it was immediately banned in both Britain and America under obscenity laws. In 1933 an American judge ruled that the book was not pornographic and could therefore not be obscene, and so from then on America became the first English-speaking country where *Ulysses* was freely available.

The Satanic Verses by SALMAN RUSHDIE   When Rushdie's fourth novel was published in 1988 it immediately caused ripples of unease among the Muslim community for its portrayal of the Prophet Muhammad. Iran's Ayatollah Khomeini issued a fatwa against Rushdie which urged Muslims to kill him over the perceived blasphemy. *The Satanic Verses* was then banned in many countries, including India, Bangladesh and Sudan, and demonstrations and public book burnings took place around the world. The issuing of the fatwa was condemned as a threat to free speech and Rushdie was forced to go into hiding for many years. Over time the controversy has died down, but to date Iran has refused to officially revoke the fatwa.

The Well of Loneliness by RADCLYFFE HALL   Published in 1928 this tale of a love affair between two women was banned in Britain after it was feared reading it could lead to an explosion of homosexuality. A court ruled that the book was an 'obscene libel' and all copies were ordered to be destroyed. It was finally published in Britain in 1949 after Hall's death, and many readers were surprised to find that the raciest scene involved two women sharing a relatively chaste kiss.

The Grapes of Wrath by JOHN STEINBECK   This tale of Depression-era farmers was published in 1939 and was banned from schools and libraries across America because of its shocking depiction of the rural poor. It is hard to imagine today why a book about the mass migration of the rural poor from Missouri, Texas and Oklahoma to California could provoke such a response, but at the time the influx and treatment of migrants was a very raw issue and Steinbeck's unflinching portrayal was perceived by some as incendiary.

THE FIRST BOOK ORDERED ON AMAZON

Today Amazon is an online shopping behemoth worth over US$300 billion, but back in 1995 it started out as an online bookstore set up in Jeff Bezos's garage in Seattle, USA. The first book ordered on Amazon was the scientific tome *Fluid Concepts and Creative Analogies: Computer Models of the Fundamental Mechanisms of Thought* by Douglas Hofstadter. The order was placed on 3 April 1995 by computer scientist John Wainwright, who was one of a handful of people who had been asked to beta-test the emerging service. Wainwright still proudly owns both the book and the packing slip that Amazon sent with it, his own tiny piece of bookselling history. *Fluid Concepts and Creative Analogies* is still available on Amazon today, some twenty years later.

MOST TRANSLATED AUTHORS

Since 1979 UNESCO has curated a list of the most translated books and authors in the world, known as the *Index Translationum*. The top ten most translated authors (1979–2016) are:

	AUTHOR	EDITIONS*
1	Agatha Christie	7,233
2	Jules Verne	4,751
3	William Shakespeare	4,281
4	Enid Blyton	3,921
5	Barbara Cartland	3,648
6	Danielle Steele	3,628
7	Vladimir Ilich Lenin	3,592
8	Hans Christian Andersen	3,520
9	Stephen King	3,354
10	Jacob Grimm	2,977

---

* listing the number of distinct translated editions.

INCUNABULA

Incunabula are early printed books or pamphlets. When Johannes Gutenberg developed moveable type (*see page 80*) it constituted a major leap forward in technology and brought huge changes to the book industry. Suddenly books which had been so time-consuming to create because they were painstakingly copied by hand, or hand printed with woodblock, could be printed in large numbers and at speed.

The first books with printed type were published *c*. 1455; all books produced in Europe between then and 1501 (an arbitrarily chosen end date) are defined as incunabula. The term was first coined by Bernhard von Mallinckrodt in 1639 when he produced a pamphlet to celebrate the bicentenary of moveable type, *De ortu et progressu artis typographicae* (*Of the rise and progress of the typographic art*). Mallinckrodt used the Latin term *incunabula*, which roughly translates as 'cradle', to describe this developing book art, at that time in its infancy.

It is thought that 28,000 editions of incunabula have survived. The British Library holds one of the largest collections: over 10,000 editions. Venice, Paris and Rome were some of the top centres of production for incunabula, which were most commonly printed in Latin.

GEORGE ORWELL'S WRITING TIPS

In his 1948 essay 'Politics and the English Language', George Orwell set out his criticism of poorly written English and offered the following valuable tips for good writing:

- ☞ Never use a metaphor, simile, or other figure of speech which you are used to seeing in print.

- ☞ Never use a long word where a short one will do.

- ☞ If it is possible to cut a word out, always cut it out.

- ☞ Never use the passive where you can use the active.

- ☞ Never use a foreign phrase, a scientific word, or a jargon word if you can think of an everyday English equivalent.

- ☞ Break any of these rules sooner than say anything outright barbarous.

CONTINUATION NOVELS

Successful and much-loved books often leave the reader wanting more and can spark the imagination of a fellow writer to predict further adventures and ultimate outcomes for our favourite characters. The following renowned books have had sequels penned by another writer:

ORIGINAL BOOK	CONTINUATION
Pride and Prejudice by Jane Austen	*Death Comes to Pemberley*[*] by P.D. James
The Hitchhiker's Guide to the Galaxy by Douglas Adams	*And Another Thing...* by Eoin Colfer
Jeeves and Wooster series by P.G. Wodehouse	*Jeeves and the Wedding Bells* by Sebastian Faulks
James Bond series by Ian Fleming	*Devil May Care* by Sebastian Faulks *Solo* by William Boyd *Colonel Sun* by Robert Markham[†]
Master of the Game saga by Sidney Sheldon	*Mistress of the Game* by Tilly Bagshawe
Millennium trilogy by Stieg Larsson	*The Girl in the Spider's Web* by David Lagercrantz
Philip Marlowe series by Raymond Chandler	*The Black-Eyed Blonde* by Benjamin Black[‡]
Sherlock Holmes mysteries by Arthur Conan Doyle	*The House of Silk* by Anthony Horowitz
Hercule Poirot mysteries by Agatha Christie	*The Monogram Murders* by Sophie Hannah

---

[*] *Pride and Prejudice* has spawned a huge number of sequels, retellings and spin-offs, so I have chosen just one by a well-known author here.

[†] Robert Markham is the pseudonym of Kingsley Amis. This 1968 continuation novel is one of the earliest by an established author.

[‡] Benjamin Black is one of the many pseudonyms of John Banville.

THE SCRIPTORIUM

Before the advent of the printing press, books were created, copied and illuminated by hand. Most were produced in monasteries by scribes, and a scriptorium (which literally means 'a place for writing' in Latin) was the dedicated room in which the scribes worked. Scriptoria were not always permanent fixtures – where a library was being created a temporary scriptorium might be established while the books for the library were copied and then repurposed once the library was fully stocked. Records from the monastery at St Albans provide evidence for a scriptorium built there in the eleventh century after Abbot Paul of Caen (1077–93) donated funds for the building. The records suggest the single-room scriptorium was built above the chapter house. The scriptorium was a place of collaboration where many monks, scribes and illuminators would work together to produce the finished manuscript – analysis of some of the medieval texts written in eleventh-century Salisbury Cathedral suggests that as many as eight different hands might have been at work on the same manuscript, sometimes switching scribes mid-sentence. Medieval scriptoria played a huge role in the creation of early books and manuscripts, but once the printing press became a reality and secular book production increased, their importance gradually faded.

The Frankfurt Book Fair (or Frankfurter Buchmesse as it is known in Germany) is the world's largest and most famous book fair and has been running for over 500 years. The book fair is essentially a trade fair where publishers, booksellers, authors and illustrators meet to sell and promote their work to an international audience.

It is thought a book fair has been held at Frankfurt since 1478 (which was just over twenty years since the very first book came off the printing presses in nearby Mainz). Indeed evidence from the Bodleian Library in Oxford suggests that Sir Thomas Bodley himself attended the Frankfurt Book Fair in the early seventeenth century to buy books for the Library.

During the eighteenth century pressure from Catholic censorship, war and competition from the book fair at Leipzig all conspired to dent the popularity of the Frankfurt Book Fair and by 1764 it was effectively shelved.

In 1949, after the end of the Second World War, the Frankfurt Book Fair was re-established as an annual event every October and before long grew to once again become the most popular book fair in the world.

Following are some statistics about the Frankfurt Book Fair:

Number of German exhibitors	2,428
	(34%)
Number of international exhibitors	4,717
	(66%)
Number of countries exhibiting	104
Number of visitors*	275,791
of whom trade visitors	170,169
and the general public	105,622

The top ten trade visitors by share of attendance[†] are:

1. Publishers
2. Booksellers
3. Librarians
4. Authors
5. Lecturers, teachers, educators
6. Designers, graphic artists, illustrators
7. Journalists
8. Universities, research institutes
9. Printers, book production
10. Editors

---

* Figures from the 2015 Book Fair.
† Figures from the 2014 Book Fair.

RECURRING CHARACTERS

It seems that some authors love a character they have created so much that they can't resist writing about them again (and again), often in a completely unrelated story. Below are several authors who use recurring characters and some of the books they appear in (naturally this is not an exhaustive list):

DAVID MITCHELL is master of this device, and frequently transports characters from one book to another, sometimes with just a walk-on role, other times as a major character. HUGO LAMB is first introduced as the flashy cousin of lead character Jason in *Black Swan Green* (2006) but later shows up as an altogether more sinister and polished version in *The Bone Clocks* (2014). Mitchell's preoccupation with the theme of reincarnation is explored through the character of MARINUS, who appears in *The Thousand Autumns of Jacob de Zoet* (2010), *The Bone Clocks* and *Slade House* (2015). LUISA REY calls into a radio station in *Ghostwritten* (1999) and returns as a reporter in *Cloud Atlas* (2004) and again in *The Bone Clocks*. Mitchell fans have delighted in spotting recurring characters in his body of work and have counted at least twenty.

STEPHEN KING likes to revisit locations as well as reuse characters and has woven a whole web of interconnected realities throughout his novels. Examples include: RANDALL FLAGG in *The Stand* (1978), *The Dark Tower* (1982), *Insomnia* (1994) and *Black House* (2001);

and in an even more random twist of the theme it is revealed in *It* (1986) that one of the children tormented by 'It', EDDIE KASPBRAK, lived next door to PAUL SHELDON's family (Paul is the protagonist of King's subsequent novel *Misery* (1987)).

KURT VONNEGUT uses the recurring character of KILGORE TROUT throughout his body of work. Trout is described as an unappreciated science-fiction author, but details of his appearance, date of birth and suchlike change from book to book. Some claim that Trout is in fact Vonnegut's alter ego. Kilgore Trout appears in *God Bless You, Mr Rosewater* (1965), *Slaughterhouse-Five* (1969), *Breakfast of Champions* (1973), *Jailbird* (1979) and *Timequake* (1997).

HARUKI MURAKAMI, more subtle in his approach, sometimes uses the reappearance of fairly minor characters in his work. Sad and unattractive USHIKAWA first appears in *The Wind-up Bird Chronicle* (1994) and then reappears in *1Q84* (2009).

BRET EASTON ELLIS uses recurring characters and locations (the liberal arts college he attended, Bennington College,* in Vermont is renamed CAMDEN COLLEGE and crops up in a number of his books).

---

* It is interesting to note that Ellis met fellow writer Donna Tartt at Bennington and she creates her own version of the college as Hampden College in *The Secret History* (1992).

Ellis's most enduring character is PATRICK BATEMAN, the main character of *American Psycho* (1991). Bateman also shows up in *The Rules of Attraction* (1987) and *Glamorama* (1998), and his brother SEAN BATEMAN appears in *The Rules of Attraction*, *The Informers* (1994) and *Lunar Park* (2005).

VELLUM

The word 'vellum' derives from the Latin word *velin* and the French word *veau*, or veal, and denotes an ancient method of producing parchment from calfskin (or occasionally lamb or kid skin). It is thought vellum grew in popularity during the Roman period from the fifth century BC onwards when the cost of importing papyrus from Egypt soared, although due to its cost and complex method of production it remained a luxury item, reserved for the best books and manuscripts. To make vellum, calfskin is soaked in lime for at least eight days to remove the hair and fat. The skin is then stretched, scraped and dried on a frame to get the vellum to a uniform thickness. As the printing press came into use in the fifteenth century, vellum continued to be used to make books; it was seen as a more luxurious and long-lasting alternative to paper. Indeed, of the forty-nine surviving copies of the first printed book, the *Gutenberg Bible* (*see page 44*), twelve are printed on vellum.

By the mid-fifteenth century the cost of paper had greatly reduced as better paper-milling processes were developed (*see page 63*). As the printing industry grew, vellum producers struggled to make enough to keep up with demand, and the more easily sourced paper swiftly took its place. Vellum was still used for bookbinding, and some early books have their original vellum covering. However, tooled leather soon became more fashionable and vellum became a niche product.

In February 2016 it was announced that the House of Lords would stop printing laws on vellum, ending a 1,000-year tradition. After an uproar the House of Lords quickly reversed its decision, citing concerns for the future of Britain's only remaining vellum producer.

MOVIES THAT STARTED LIFE AS BOOKS

Many famous books have been directly adapted into films, with varying success. However, less well known are the novels, works of non-fiction, short stories and children's books that have provided inspiration for film-makers to create a movie more loosely based on the work. The following films were all inspired by books:

DIE HARD (1988)   This hugely popular movie was inspired by the 1979 thriller *Nothing Lasts Forever* by Roderick Thorp.

Rambo: First Blood (1982)   The book *First Blood* by David Morrell (1972) inspired this movie about a Vietnam War veteran on the run. As with many adaptations the plot was tinkered with in the film version.

The Parent Trap (1961)   The original Disney film was based on the German book *Das doppelte Lottchen* (titled *Lottie and Lisa* in the English version) by Erich Kästner (1940).

Full Metal Jacket (1987)   Stanley Kubrick adapted (and rearranged) the novel *The Short-Timers* by Gustav Hasford (1979) into his iconic Vietnam War-era picture.

Mean Girls (2004)   This movie about teenage cliques in American high schools is largely based on the non-fiction self-help tome *Queen Bees & Wannabes: Helping your Daughter Survive Cliques, Gossip, Boyfriends & Other Realities of Adolescence* by Rosalind Wiseman (2002).

Clueless (1995)   This classic teen comedy flick was loosely based on *Emma* by Jane Austen (1815).

Slumdog Millionaire (2008)   An Oscar-winning film based on the book *Q & A* by Vikas Swarup (2005).

Million Dollar Baby (2004)   Based on a collection of short stories *Rope Burns: Stories from the Corner* by F.X. Toole (aka boxing trainer Jerry Boyd) (2000).

BABE (1995)   Adapted from the much-loved children's book *The Sheep-Pig* by Dick King-Smith (1983).

PSYCHO (1960)   Alfred Hitchcock's seminal horror movie was based on a book with the same title by Robert Bloch published in 1959.[*]

GOODFELLAS (1990)   Adapted from *Wiseguy* by Nicholas Pileggi (1986).

BLADE RUNNER (1982)   Inspired by Philip K. Dick's *Do Androids Dream of Electric Sheep?* (1968).

THE SOCIAL NETWORK (2010)   Based on the non-fiction *The Accidental Billionaires: The Founding of Facebook, A Tale of Sex, Money, Genius, and Betrayal* by Ben Mezrich (2009).

IT'S A WONDERFUL LIFE (1946)   Based on a short story 'The Greatest Gift' by Philip Van Doren Stern (1943).

---

[*] Hitchcock was so keen to keep the plot twists secret that he attempted to buy up every copy of the book.

THE FIRST BOOK PRINTED IN ENGLISH:
RECUYELL OF THE HISTORIES OF TROYE

William Caxton (*c.* 1422–1492) was a pioneer of book printing and it was he who produced the first book printed in the English language.

Recuyell of the Histories of Troye by Raoul Lefèvre was originally written in Latin, the language in which the majority of early books were printed. Caxton thought that because the ancient heroes of Troy were said to be the ancestors of the Burgundian dukes, translating the work into English would make a fine gift for the Duke of Burgundy's new wife, Margaret of York, sister to the English king, Edward IV.

Caxton spent three years translating the work and then, inspired by the early printed books he encountered in Cologne, decided to break with tradition: instead of having the text written and illustrated by a scribe, he had the book printed.

At this time very few books had been printed in any language other than Latin; a few texts had been printed in Italian, such as Boccaccio's *Decameron* in *c.*1470, and a couple of Bibles had been printed in the German language. In 1473 Caxton set up a printing press in Flanders (both Ghent and Bruges have been suggested as likely locations) to print the book. Only eighteen copies are known to survive today, one of which was recently sold at auction for over £1 million.

A BRIEF HISTORY OF
COPYRIGHT IN THE UK

The concept of copyright can be seen as originating with the Stationers' Company (the guild of manuscript writers, printers and illuminators; *see page 52*), which during the fifteenth century held a virtual monopoly on book production. Because of this, those wishing to sell a book needed to register their right to do so with the Company. The register of works kept by the Stationers' Company allowed printers and writers to produce their work exclusively for a set period of time in a de facto early notion of copyright.

The origin of copyright law comes from the Statute of Anne, first passed in 1709, which gave copyright not to the publisher but to the author for a period of fourteen years. This was the first copyright law passed anywhere in the world and laid the foundation for intellectual property rights. Separate pieces of legislation were passed to protect the copyright of music and artworks. In 1911 a new, all-encompassing law was passed: the Copyright Act 1911. The Act saw copyright extended to the period of the author's, artist's or musician's life plus fifty years. Copyright law was further defined and updated by the Copyright, Designs and Patents Act 1988, which covers writers, musicians, artists and others. Amending legislation to the Act extended the period of copyright to seventy years from the end of the year in which the creator of the work dies.

SOME LITERARY MOVEMENTS OF NOTE

ROMANTICISM Movement of the eighteenth and nineteenth centuries, most notably in poetry. The ethos included a rejection of the power of reason and a yearning for an idealized, pastoral past. Some key players: William Wordsworth (1770–1850), Samuel Taylor Coleridge (1772–1834), George Gordon, Lord Byron (1788–1824), Percy Bysshe Shelley (1792–1822) and Victor Hugo (1802–1885).

TRANSCENDENTALISM An exclusively American idealistic movement in the mid-nineteenth century concerned with expressing the inner spirit and freeing the mind from daily drudgery. Some key players: Ralph Waldo Emerson (1803–1882), Margaret Fuller (1810–1850) and Henry David Thoreau (1817–1862).

REALISM The realist movement sought to report life as it happened, recording minute details and telling a story with no judgement. This gave rise to novels more concerned with character than plot. Some key players: Honoré de Balzac (1799–1850), Charles Dickens (1812–1870), George Eliot (1819–1880), Gustave Flaubert (1821–1880) and Leo Tolstoy (1828–1910).

NATURALISM The logical progression of the realist movement, naturalism moved away from the idea of free will and posited that characters were victims of their social environment. A naturalist novel is written in an almost documentary style, reporting on characters without comment. Some key players: Émile Zola (1840–1902), Edith Wharton (1862–1937) and Stephen Crane (1871–1900).

MODERNISM   Emerged with the start of the twentieth century and saw a move towards embracing individualism and experimentation in a direct challenge to the former Victorian way of thinking. Some key players: Virginia Woolf (1882–1941), Ezra Pound (1885–1972), T.S. Eliot (1888–1965) and F. Scott Fitzgerald (1896–1940).

EXISTENTIALISM   Often portrayed as a negative way of looking at life, concerned as it is with an individual finding their own meaning in life. In literary terms existentialism is sometimes expressed through the absurdity of life with characters caught up in situations beyond their control. Some key players: Fyodor Dostoyevsky (1821–1881), Franz Kafka (1883–1924) and Albert Camus (1913–1960).

POSTMODERNISM   Partly a reaction to modernism, shaped by a distrust of ideologies, self-consciousness about the creative process and the idea that nothing is original as everything has already been done before. This liberates writers to be inspired by, and play with, old ideas and themes, revisiting them in a fresh, and frequently radical, way. Some key players: Iris Murdoch (1919–1999), Doris Lessing (1919–2013), Kurt Vonnegut (1922–2007), John Ashbery (1927–), John Barth (1930–), Geoffrey Hill (1932–2016).

LITERARY FAMILIES

Sometimes it seems that literary talent might flow in the blood. The following are all famous literary families:

CHARLOTTE (1816–1855), EMILY (1818–1848) and ANNE BRONTË (1820–1849) were literary siblings most famous for *Jane Eyre* (1847), *Wuthering Heights* (1847) and *The Tenant of Wildfell Hall* (1848) respectively.

MARY WOLLSTONECRAFT (1759–1797) was a writer and philosopher, most famous for *A Vindication of the Rights of Woman* (1792). She was married to the radical philosopher WILLIAM GODWIN (1756–1836) and had a daughter MARY SHELLEY (1797–1851), who famously wrote *Frankenstein* (1818) and was married to Romantic poet PERCY BYSSHE SHELLEY (1792–1822).

Booker Prize-winning writer and poet A.S. BYATT (1936–) is sister to novelist MARGARET DRABBLE (1939–). According to newspaper reports, the sisters have apparently been estranged since childhood due to their intense sibling rivalry and are said not to read each other's books due to the autobiographical elements in their work.

KINGSLEY AMIS (1922–1995) and his son MARTIN AMIS (1949–) both featured in *The Times*'s list of the top fifty greatest British writers since 1945. Kingsley was an extremely prolific writer and wrote over twenty novels, numerous collections of poetry, television and radio scripts and a memoir. Martin, though less prolific, is no less lauded as a voice of his generation.

JACOB (1785–1863) and WILHELM GRIMM (1786–1859), better known as THE BROTHERS GRIMM worked together for many years collecting, preserving and rewriting popular folk tales.

Italian poet GABRIELE ROSSETTI (1783–1854) had four children, each of whom had varying success in the arts. CHRISTINA ROSSETTI (1830–1894) found fame as a poet; DANTE GABRIEL ROSSETTI (1828–1882) as an artist, illustrator and poet; WILLIAM MICHAEL ROSSETTI (1829–1919) as a critic; and MARIA FRANCESCA ROSSETTI (1827–1876) as a writer. Their uncle was JOHN WILLIAM POLIDORI (1795–1821), doctor to Lord Byron and author of the first vampire story in English *The Vampyre* (1819).

UNFINISHED NOVELS

A novel may be unfinished for a number of reasons: the death of an author, a change of direction or simply writer's block. The following are all works by famous authors that were left unfinished:

The Mystery of Edwin Drood by Charles Dickens   Dickens died in 1870 aged 58 and left this book almost exactly half-written: he produced six of the planned twelve monthly instalments. Unfortunately he did not leave notes on the book's ending, so although many have attempted to complete the whodunnit, no one knows what outcome Dickens intended.

Wives and Daughters by Elizabeth Gaskell   Gaskell was publishing this novel in instalments in *Cornhill Magazine* but died in 1865 before it could be concluded. Fortunately journalist Frederick Greenwood stepped in to take the story to its logical conclusion.

The Mysterious Stranger by Mark Twain   In his lifetime, Twain had worked on three different draft versions of this novel, all focused on a character named Satan. In 1916, six years after Twain's death, the three versions were woven together and published, but to little critical acclaim.

Sanditon by Jane Austen   Austen's last novel was only eleven chapters in when she died in 1817. Set in the new seaside resort of Sanditon, the opening seemed to offer countless opportunities for the story, and many Austen fans have subsequently attempted to complete the novel with varying degrees of success.

The Original of Laura by Vladimir Nabokov   When Nabokov died in 1977 he left express instructions that any ongoing work be destroyed. However, Nabokov's son couldn't quite bring himself to obey his father's wishes and instead kept a fragmentary manuscript in a bank vault for many years before finally publishing it in 2009.

The Last Tycoon by F. Scott Fitzgerald   Inspired by Hollywood mogul Irving Thalberg, Fitzgerald's last book had seventeen of the planned thirty-one chapters written by the time of his death in 1940. Fitzgerald's friend Edmund Wilson edited and published the work in 1941.

The First Man by Albert Camus   Camus was working on this autobiographical novel when he was killed in a car crash in 1960. The muddied manuscript was found among the wreckage of the car and recovered. Camus's daughter transcribed the unfinished novel and it was published in 1994.

The Trial by Franz Kafka   When Kafka died in 1924 after years of illness he left the majority of his works unfinished and ordered that they be destroyed. His wishes were ignored and many of his incomplete novels were later published. *The Trial* is one of Kafka's most acclaimed novels; although it was unpolished and in-complete, he had at least written the final chapter so the ending was his own.

Answered Prayers by Truman Capote   Capote signed a lucrative contract for *Answered Prayers* in 1966 but continued to fail to deliver it as his career took off after the success of *In Cold Blood* and he became lost in sub-stance and alcohol abuse. After critics began to doubt his intention ever to publish the novel he released four chapters as a work-in-progress to *Vanity Fair* in 1975. Unfortunately the thinly veiled and unflattering portrayal of many of his friends in the extracts caused Capote to be ostracized, and the novel remained unfinished. It was finally published as a fragment in 1984.

FIRST BOOK PRINTED IN BRITISH AMERICA: THE *BAY PSALM BOOK*

The Whole Booke of Psalmes Faithfully Translated into English Metre, or *Bay Psalm Book*, was the first book to be printed in the new colony of America, in 1640. To print the book a printing press, paper, type and a printer were imported from England. Unfortunately the man tasked with printing the book, the Reverend Jose Glover, died on the voyage and so his wife Elizabeth established the press herself in Cambridge, Massachusetts. Glover's apprentice, Stephen Daye (1594?–1668), was entrusted with printing the book – Daye was actually a locksmith by profession; his spelling and typographical skills were inconsistent at best. However, he managed to print an estimated 1,700 copies of the religious work, which were sold for 20 pence each. Today only eleven known copies survive and when one came to auction in 2013 at Sotheby's in New York it reached a record-breaking $14 million, becoming the most expensive book ever sold at auction. The only copy of the *Bay Psalm Book* to survive outside of North America is held at the Bodleian Library in Oxford (Arch. G e.40).

YOUNGEST DEBUT WRITERS

Some precocious talents have written and published books at a very young age, proving that successful writing does not always spring from experience. Below is the age of some notable writers when their first book was published:

WRITER	TITLE	AGE
S.E. Hinton	*The Outsiders* (1967)*	18
Françoise Sagan	*Bonjour Tristesse* (1954)	18
Percy Bysshe Shelley	*Zastrozzi* (1810)	18
Susan Hill	*The Enclosure* (1961)†	18
Matthew Lewis	*The Monk* (1796)	19
Mary Shelley	*Frankenstein* (1818)‡	21
Brett Easton Ellis	*Less Than Zero* (1985)	21
Daisy Ashford	*The Young Visiters* (1919)§	37

---

* Susan Hinton began writing *The Outsiders* when she was just 15. When the novel was published she was lauded as the voice of her generation and it was made into a major movie.

† Hill was just 15 when she started writing *The Enclosure*. Because it included a married couple it was considered an unsuitable writing subject for a schoolgirl and caused a minor scandal on publication.

‡ Shelley was only 18 years old when she began work on *Frankenstein*, but it was not published until she was 21.

§ Daisy Ashford wrote *The Young Visiters* when she was just 9 years old. However, it was not published until Daisy was 37 and had rediscovered the charming manuscript. The book was deliberately printed with Ashford's original spellings and poor punctuation to preserve the childish voice. *The Young Visiters* was so popular that it went through eight reprints in its first year.

A SHORT HISTORY OF BOOK FONTS

The first fonts were created by Johannes Gutenberg when he developed the first printing press with moveable type in the 1400s. Based upon the hand-drawn calligraphy used by scribes at the time, the first fonts are known as black-letter or Gothic fonts and use angled lines and tall and narrow letters. These fonts can be hard for the modern reader to decipher.* Black-letter fonts are still used for the mastheads of some newspapers such as *The New York Times*. A modern Gothic style font is:

𝔉𝔯𝔞𝔨𝔱𝔲𝔯

In the 1460s/70s more legible fonts came to the fore, based upon the writing style of Italian humanists; these became known as Humanist or Venetian type. During this period Nicolas Jenson developed the first roman typeface. Humanist fonts feature small letter height and relatively dark type style. A classic Humanist typeface is:

Jenson

In the 1490s Old Style type, a serif style of typeface based on Roman inscriptions, was introduced. Old Style

---

* Black-letter typefaces fell out of fashion across the world but remained popular in Germany, finally being largely replaced with sans serif fonts (*see page 118*) in the 1920s. However, during the 1930s when the Nazi Party rose to power, Hitler began to look back to old font styles and initially encouraged the use of black-letter fonts, describing Fraktur as *Volk*, which basically meant it was to be regarded as 'the people's font'.

fonts are much more refined, probably in part due to the developing skills of the punchcutters (the person responsible for cutting out the moulds from which the types were cast), with greater contrast between thick and thin strokes. In 1501 the first italic font was developed from the Old Style fonts and was used where space was at a premium. A classic Old Style font is:

Garamond

Old Style fonts have retained their popularity and are still some of the most commonly used fonts, especially in book publishing.

At the end of the seventeenth century the Transitional (or Neoclassical) fonts were developed. The first fonts of this type were much further removed from handwriting than Humanist or even Old Style fonts, with a narrower stroke and thinner serifs, allowing more white space on the page. A classic Transitional font is:

Baskerville

Baskerville was developed by English printer and typefounder John Baskerville in 1757. It was not immediately popular in England, but in 1758 Baskerville met Benjamin Franklin, who much admired the design and took samples of Baskerville back to America to be used in federal government publishing.

In the late eighteenth century Modern or Didone typefaces were developed. This style took the high contrast between thick and thin strokes to an extreme and included even thinner serifs. The classic Modern font was developed by Giambattista Bodoni in the late eighteenth century:

Bodoni

In the 1800s the slab serif was introduced, which was a stronger font style for use in adverts, billboards and posters. Because this was used just for short bursts of text in large sizes it was generally only used for display texts.

As technology in printing improved so too did font styles diversify, with the introduction of sans serif (*see page 118*) fonts. Manual typesetting became redundant and industrialization meant that new fonts were easier to develop and distribute. Some contemporary fonts of note are the geometric sans serif font **Futura**, developed in the 1920s, and the now ubiquitous sans serif font **Helvetica**, designed in 1957.

MOST PROLIFIC WRITERS

Stephen King pondered those authors who penned just a couple of books in their writing careers and quipped 'what did they do with the rest of their time?' King has written some sixty full-length novels and more than 200 short stories over his lifetime so far, but his output pales in comparison with the following incredibly prolific authors:

Spanish writer CORÍN TELLADO (1927–2009) wrote over 4,000 romance novels in her 63-year writing career, which sold in excess of 400 million copies in Spain and Latin America.

KATHLEEN LINDSAY (1903–1973) used eleven different pseudonyms to pen some 904 romance novels over her lifetime.

Well-known children's author ENID BLYTON (1897–1968) wrote over 800 books during her career, which have been translated into ninety languages and sold over 600 million copies.

Dame BARBARA CARTLAND (1901–2000) is most famous for her romance novels, but she also penned plays, cookbooks and poetry. Cartland produced 723 novels over her career.

English crime and science-fiction writer JOHN CREASEY (1908–1973) reportedly received over 750 rejection letters before finally getting published. Once published he did not stop, racking up over 600 books and using twenty-eight pseudonyms.

GEORGES SIMENON (1903–1989) penned nearly 500 books during his lifetime. The Belgian writer's most famous creation was the detective Jules Maigret.

Biochemistry professor ISAAC ASIMOV (1920–1972) wrote many influential sci-fi classics and produced nearly 500 books in total.

QUILLS

Quills as writing implements were developed around the sixth century AD and quickly superseded the reed pen or metal stylus as the implement of choice for the writing of books.

The best quills were taken from the flight feathers of live birds, plucked in the spring from the left wing (because the feathers curved away, making it easier for a right-handed scribe to use). Goose feathers were most commonly used but swan feathers were considered superior, in part due to their rarity; the feathers of crows were used for making fine lines.

The feathers were first dipped in hot sand in order to make the tips hard; the plume was then trimmed away and the tip sharpened to a point with a thin slit up the centre, much like a modern fountain pen.

Quill pens needed regular sharpening with a knife (hence the origin of the term penknife) and if heavily used lasted only about a week before they had to be discarded. John of Tilbury, a scholar in the household of Thomas Becket in the twelfth century, described how a scribe taking a full day of dictation would need between sixty and a hundred quills sharpened and readied.

THE MAKING OF A BIBLE
IN THE MIDDLE AGES

In the Middle Ages making a book was a long and labour-intensive task involving many skilled crafts-people. To produce a Bible written on vellum (*see page 23*), the skins of roughly 170 calves were needed. The skins were then immersed in lime and water for between three and ten days, with regular stirring, in order to dissolve the hair and fat. Once most of the hair was removed, the skin was washed and then stretched out to dry on a frame; it was then further scraped to remove any last residues of hair and fat and to ensure it was of a uniform thickness. The vellum was pegged and stretched onto a frame to dry, with the pegs regularly tightened to keep the parchment taut. Once dried, the vellum could be trimmed to size and was usually cut twice as big as the desired book size so that it could be folded into a quire of, for example, four leaves and bound together with further quires to assemble the book. The skins were then rubbed with pumice to smooth the surface and finally a layer of chalk was applied to enable the vellum to take the ink without running.

Before writing could commence the scribe (or scribes) had to begin the laborious task of marking out lines on every page; this was done by scoring the skin with a sharp instrument or alternatively by marking lines with lead. A reed pen, metal stylus or quill (*see page 41*) was used for writing; inks (*see page 73*) were made from natural materials such as minerals, plants and berries. The scribe would sit at an angled desk to make writing easier; with the original text and copy side by side, the vellum was weighted down to prevent it from rolling up. In the Middle Ages writing was a two-handed affair: in one hand the quill or stylus would be held; in the other a knife – for sharpening the quill, scrubbing out mistakes and keeping place in the text. Once the scribe had completed copying out a Bible it would be given to the illuminator to embellish and illustrate the text using elaborate coloured pigments and gold or silver leaf. Finally the book would be sewn together and bound, with wooden covers, perhaps covered in tooled leather.

BOOK SUPERLATIVES

SMALLEST BOOK IN THE WORLD   The world's smallest book, *Teeny Ted from Turnip Town*, was written in 2007 by Malcolm Douglas Chaplin and was printed on pure crystalline silicon using a gallium-ion beam by his brother Robert, at Simon Fraser University in British Columbia, Canada. The tiny 30-page work is so small it could fit on the width of a human hair, measuring 70 micrometres by 100 micrometres, and can only be read using an electron microscope.

LARGEST BOOK IN THE WORLD   According to the *Guinness Book of Records* the world's largest book is a

2012 text on the Prophet Muhammad produced in Dubai. It measures an impressive 500 cm × 806 cm and weighs a hefty 1,500 kg. It took over fifty people to create the 42-page work.

LONGEST BOOK IN THE WORLD   *Artamène ou le Grand Cyrus* (*Atarmene or Cyrus the Great*), a seventeenth-century romantic novel by Madeleine de Scudéry, is the longest book in the world. The ten-volume work is 2.1 million words long and has 13,095 pages.

MOST EXPENSIVE BOOK IN THE WORLD   Bill Gates paid an astonishing $30.8 million in 1994 for Leonardo da Vinci's *Codex Leicester*. The hand-drawn manuscript was compiled by Renaissance polymath and artist Leonardo da Vinci between 1506 and 1510 and is one of only thirty of his notebooks still in existence. The *Codex* contains sketches, notes and ideas on a diverse range of subjects, giving scholars a rare glimpse into the mind of a genius.

MOST VALUABLE BOOK IN THE WORLD   The *Gutenberg Bible* is probably the most valuable printed book in the world; in one sense it can be considered priceless, as all complete copies are owned by institutions and so unlikely ever to come up for sale. The *Gutenberg Bible* was the first book to be printed in *c.*1455 using modern moveable type, a process which revolutionised the book trade. Only 180 were originally printed, of which only 49 survive today and of these only 21 are complete. Nearly all the surviving Gutenberg Bibles are owned by museums, institutions or libraries.

RAREST BOOK IN THE WORLD   A 1593 first edition of *Venus and Adonis*, William Shakespeare's first published work, held by the Bodleian Library in Oxford, is the only known copy of this book in existence, making it one of the rarest printed books in the world (Arch. G e.31 (2)).

BESTSELLING WORK OF FICTION OF ALL TIME   The bestselling novel of all time is Charles Dickens's *A Tale of Two Cities*. Published in 1859 the classic book has sold an incredible 200 million copies worldwide.

BESTSELLING NON-FICTION BOOK OF ALL TIME   The Bible is the bestselling book of all time, selling an estimated 5 billion copies worldwide. The Bible was the first book off the printing press (*see Gutenberg Bible above*) in *c.* 1455 and has since been translated into over 394 languages.

BIGGEST PUBLISHING HOUSE   Penguin Random House is the world's largest general trade publisher; Pearson, publishing academic and educational books, is the overall largest book publisher.

OLDEST PUBLISHING HOUSE   Cambridge University Press (*see page 57*), established in 1534, is the world's oldest publishing house. Until recently the oldest independent publishing house was John Murray, established in 1768; it was bought by Hodder Headline in 2002.

FAMOUS OPENING LINES

The first few lines of a book are supposed to draw a reader in and pique their interest. Many writers have come up with some truly memorable opening lines (although not all are memorable for the right reasons), a selection of which are below:

'It was a bright cold day in April,
and the clocks were striking thirteen.'
Nineteen Eighty-Four (1949)
by George Orwell

'Last night I dreamt I went to Manderley again.'
Rebecca (1938) by Daphne du Maurier

'It is a truth universally acknowledged,
that a single man in possession of a good fortune,
must be in want of a wife.'
Pride and Prejudice (1813) by Jane Austen

'It was the best of times, it was the worst of times.'
A Tale of Two Cities (1859) by Charles Dickens

'I had the story, bit by bit, from various people,
and, as generally happens in such cases,
each time it was a different story.'
Ethan Frome (1911) by Edith Wharton

'Call me Ishmael.'
Moby-Dick (1851) by Herman Melville

'All happy families are alike;
each unhappy family is unhappy in its own way.'
Anna Karenina (1878) by Leo Tolstoy

'The past is a foreign country:
they do things differently there.'
The Go-Between by L.P. Hartley (1953)

'Miss Brooke had that kind of beauty which seems
to be thrown into relief by poor dress.'
Middlemarch (1871) by George Eliot

'Under certain circumstance there are few hours in
life more agreeable than the hour dedicated to the
ceremony known as afternoon tea.'
The Portrait of a Lady (1880) by Henry James

'It was a dark and stormy night; the rain fell in
torrents, except at occasional intervals, when
it was checked by a violent gust of wind which
swept up the streets.'
Paul Clifford (1830) by Edward George Bulwer-Lytton

'You better not never tell nobody but God.'
The Color Purple (1982) by Alice Walker

'He was an old man who fished alone in a skiff
in the Gulf Stream and he had gone eighty-four
days now without taking a fish.'
The Old Man and the Sea (1952)
by Ernest Hemingway

ALTERNATIVE BOOK TITLES

When books are published in different territories the title sometimes needs to be changed to better fit the local market. The following famous books have been published in the USA with an alternative title:

ORIGINAL TITLE	ALTERNATIVE TITLE
Harry Potter and the Philosopher's Stone by J.K. Rowling	*Harry Potter and the Sorcerer's Stone*
Northern Lights by Philip Pullman	*The Golden Compass*
Notre-Dame de Paris by Victor Hugo	*The Hunchback of Notre-Dame*
Cider with Rosie by Laurie Lee	*The Edge of Day*
Aunts Aren't Gentleman by P.G. Wodehouse*	*The Cat-nappers*
Five Little Pigs by Agatha Christie*	*Murder in Retrospect*
The Iron Man by Ted Hughes	*The Iron Giant*
The Sheep-Pig by Dick King-Smith	*Babe the Gallant Pig*
Casino Royale† by Ian Fleming	*You Asked for It*

---

* Both P.G. Wodehouse and Agatha Christie had numerous book titles changed for the American market.

† The US edition of *Casino Royale* was originally published in 1954 but did not sell well; when it was published in paperback by American Popular Library it was retitled *You Asked for It*. Curiously they also changed the name of the famous hero to Jimmy Bond.

SIGNED BOOKS

A book signed by the author always adds to its value, but there are many different types of author signature, some more sought after than others:

SIGNED BOOKS   A book signed by its author is generally considered a good thing and enhances the value of a book. A dated signature (especially if the date was close to the publication date) is even more sought after.

INSCRIBED BOOKS   Sometimes also known as presentation copies, these book are dedicated to a particular individual. For some a book inscription adds to the charm of a book, but for others owning a book dedicated to someone else holds no charm at all.

ASSOCIATION COPY   These are some of the most valuable types of book signature. An association copy is a book with a personal dedication by the author to another famous person connected to the book or author; for example, a copy of Harold Pinter's *The Homecoming* inscribed to the lead actress in the play, his wife Vivien Merchant.

DEDICATION COPY   This is the holy grail of book signatures due to their rarity, a book signed by the author and inscribed with the name of the person to whom the book is dedicated in print.

THE DETECTION CLUB

In 1930 detective writer Anthony Berkeley set up the Detection Club. The Club was a forum for mystery writers to meet and discuss writing, and to this end held regular dinners in London. The club's first president was G.K. Chesterton, and founding members included:

Dorothy L. Sayers | Agatha Christie | Freeman Wills Crofts | Austin Freeman | Jessie Rikard

The Club created a list of ethics to try to ensure their mysteries were solvable and fair to the reading public. They also composed an oath which reflected the Club's ethics:

Do you promise that your detectives shall well and truly detect the crimes presented to them using those wits which it may please you to bestow upon them and not placing reliance on nor making use of Divine Revelation, Feminine Intuition, Mumbo Jumbo, Jiggery-Pokery, Coincidence, or Act of God?

During the golden age of detective writing Club members wrote a number of mystery novels in collaboration, each writing a chapter or two – the most notable being *The Floating Admiral*, which was published in 1931 and included a different resolution to the mystery written by each of the contributors. The Club still meets; its current president is Martin Edwards.

ISBN

An International Standard Book Number (ISBN) is a code used to identify every individual edition of a work – each hardback, paperback, audiobook and e-book has a different ISBN. The system is international and ensures authors, booksellers, libraries and publishers can identify the varying editions of a work and market it accordingly. The idea of Standard Book Numbering (SBN) was developed in 1965 by Gordon Foster, professor of statistics at Trinity College, Dublin, and was initially a nine-digit code. In 1967 the code was adapted to become ISBN by David Whitaker and Emery Koltay and was then adopted by the International Organization of Standardization (ISO) as ISO 2018 in 1970, whereupon it became a ten-digit code. As the system has grown and been adopted worldwide the ISBN code has been extended once again, and since 2007 it has had thirteen digits. The code breaks down thus:

- ☞ The first three digits are a standard prefix, currently 978 or 979.
- ☞ The next group of between one and five digits relates to the geographical area of the publishers.
- ☞ The next group of digits identifies the publisher or imprint.
- ☞ The following group of digits indicates the edition and format of a specific title.
- ☞ The final digit is a 'check digit' which makes the ISBN valid.

There are over 160 ISBN agencies worldwide, each of which provides ISBNs to a certain geographical region. In the United Kingdom the private company Nielsen Book Services generates all ISBNs for UK publishers; in America another private company, R.R. Bowker, issues ISBNs for US publishers.

THE STATIONERS' COMPANY

In the fifteenth century, when printed book production was in its infancy, manuscript writers, bookbinders and illuminators began to group together around St Paul's Cathedral in London, where they set up their stalls or 'stations' to ply their trade. At this time most tradespeople were itinerant but because these trades occupied 'stationary' stalls they became known as stationers. Thus in 1403 when they decided to establish a guild, the name Stationers' Company was selected.

When the printing press was introduced in the mid-fifteenth century the Stationers immediately embraced the new technology and became pioneers in this burgeoning industry in the UK. In 1557 the Stationers' Company was granted a royal charter, which allowed it almost a monopoly over book printing in the United Kingdom as only those who were members of the guild or who had been granted royal privileges could print any matter for sale in the UK. The Stationers went on to develop the early model for copyright (*see page 28*), whereby a publisher or individual might register a book with the Stationers' Company for a small fee and would then have the right to publish that title for a set number of years.

In 1610 the Company signed an agreement with Sir Thomas Bodley to supply a copy of every book published in the UK to the Bodleian Library in what was the beginning of legal deposit (*see page 95*). Today the Stationers' Company includes members from all sectors of the communication industries – publishers, papermakers, newspapers, broadcast and online media – and hosts events, talks and seminars for its 900 members.

PUBLISHING REJECTIONS

It has become something of a cliché for a writer to face many rejections before finally getting into print, as if it is this painful process that makes their ultimate success all the sweeter. The authors below were all rejected numerous times before finally finding success, proving that it is worth persisting:

BEATRIX POTTER   Potter received so many rejections for *The Tale of Peter Rabbit* that she went on to publish 250 copies herself, a move which finally caught the attention of a publisher. She subsequently sold over 45 million copies.

L.M. MONTGOMERY   Her debut novel *Anne of Green Gables* was rejected by five different publishers before being picked up by L.C. Page & Company and going on to sell over 50 million copies.

MARGARET MITCHELL   *Gone with the Wind* was rejected by thirty-eight different publishers before finally securing a deal and selling 30 million copies.

YANN MARTEL   The Booker Prize-winning *The Life of Pi* was rejected by five London publishers.

JAMES JOYCE   *Dubliners* was rejected twenty-two times before finally securing a small print run (in its first year only 379 copies were sold and Joyce bought 120 of them himself).

JAMES PATTERSON   *The Thomas Berryman Number* was rejected by thirty-one publishers before finally securing a deal. Patterson has since sold over 220 million books.

J.K. ROWLING   Rowling's agent received rejections from twelve publishers before the eight-year-old daughter of an editor at Bloomsbury voiced her love of the manuscript and *Harry Potter and the Philosopher's Stone* finally was published.

WILLIAM GOLDING   *Lord of the Flies* was rejected over twenty times before it got published.

THE OLDEST BOOKSHOP IN THE UK

The oldest continuously trading bookshop in the UK is at 1 Trinity Street in Cambridge. The shop first opened its doors as a bookseller in 1581; before this from 1537 the site was occupied by Spierinck, a bookbinder. The shop has traded under a number of names since then, including as Bowes & Bowes from 1907 to 1953, when the firm was bought out by W.H. Smith. Since 1992 the bookshop has been the main bookshop of Cambridge University Press.

PENGUIN PAPERBACKS

In 1934 Allen Lane was travelling back from a weekend in Devon with his friend Agatha Christie and was frustrated to find that the bookshop at the station had nothing worth reading in it. This got Lane thinking, and he soon came up with the concept of creating cheap paperback version of classic quality fiction and non-fiction, devoid of ornamentation and costing just sixpence each (the cost of a pack of ten cigarettes at the time).

Lane took his idea to his employer at the publishing house Bodley Head but they were not keen, as paperbacks at that time were generally only used for trashy penny dreadfuls or pulp fiction. However, they reluctantly allowed him to work on the idea in his spare time.

Lane recruited his brothers Dick and John to the endeavour, and together they came up with the name for their imprint, Penguin Books. They engaged a young designer named Edward Young and sent him off to London Zoo to sketch some penguins and soon he had created the now iconic Penguin logo. The covers were kept plain and simple to keep costs down, with the type set in Gill Sans. The simple jacket colours were as follows:

JACKET COLOUR	TYPE OF BOOK
orange	fiction
green	crime fiction
blue	non-fiction
cerise	travel and adventure
dark blue	biography
red	drama
purple	essays
yellow	miscellaneous

The first ten authors picked for the launch of Penguin paperbacks were:

Agatha Christie | Susan Ertz | Ernest Hemingway
Eric Linklater | Compton Mackenzie
André Maurois | Beverly Nichols
Dorothy L. Sayers | Mary Webb | E.H. Young

Once the books were ready for launch in 1935, Lane was vindicated when Woolworths put in an order for 63,500 copies, and within weeks all the titles needed to be reprinted. After just one year of trading Penguin had sold over 3 million books.

During the Second World War the Penguin paperback really took off, as they were light enough and cheap enough to fit in a soldier's back pocket and their simple design meant the production of the books could adapt easily to the restrictions of rationing.

In 1938 America adopted the paperback model and introduced pocket books with their first title *The Good Earth* by Pearl S. Buck. It is not an exaggeration to say that Allen Lane's paperbacks revolutionized the publishing industry, making quality books easily affordable to all.

THE OLDEST PUBLISHING HOUSE IN THE WORLD

Cambridge University Press (CUP) proudly holds the title of being both the oldest printer and the oldest publishing house in the world. It was established by letters patent issued by Henry VIII in 1534, but due to tussles with the Stationers' Company in London (*see page 52*), which believed it should have a monopoly on printing books, the Press did not print its first book (*Two Treatises of the Lord His Holie Supper*) until 1584; it has been continuously printing books since then.

The first practising University printer was Thomas Thomas, who was appointed in 1583, but it was his successor John Legate who started printing Bibles, the first Cambridge Bible being a copy of the Geneva Bible, published in 1591. Since then CUP has published many different editions of the Bible, including the 1763 Folio Bible published by John Baskerville using his own type design, which is regarded as one of the finest Bible printings of all time.

Today CUP publishes not only Bibles but also textbooks, reference works and over 240 scholarly journals.

IDENTIFYING A FIRST EDITION

A true first edition is the first print run of a book. A book does not become a second (or subsequent) edition until it has been reprinted with changes to the typesetting – perhaps substantial corrections have been made, a foreword added or suchlike. If all copies of a first edition sell out and a publisher reprints the book without major changes then these copies are still considered first editions but would be referred to as 'first edition, second printing'.

Unfortunately there are no hard and fast rules for publishers on how to indicate a first edition. Some of the ways a first edition can be identified as follows:

- ☞ The date on the title page is the same as the date on the imprint page.
- ☞ The imprint page includes the words 'first edition', 'first impression', 'first published' or 'first printing'.
- ☞ Since the 1940s many publishers have printed a number line on the imprint page of a book. Number lines do not follow a set style, sometimes ascending, sometimes descending, but if the book is a first edition the number line will contain the number one. Here are some examples of number lines for first editions:

$$1 \quad 2 \quad 3 \quad 4 \quad 5 \quad 6 \quad 7 \quad 8 \quad 9$$
$$9 \quad 8 \quad 7 \quad 6 \quad 5 \quad 4 \quad 3 \quad 2 \quad 1$$
$$1 \quad 3 \quad 5 \quad 7 \quad 9 \quad 2 \quad 4 \quad 6 \quad 8$$

When printing the second edition the publisher would remove the '1' from the number line, leaving '2' as the lowest number, indicating that it is a second edition, and so on, removing the lowest number each time the book is reprinted.

Ultimately, correctly identifying a first edition can be extremely troublesome, and it may be wise to consult an expert.

SOME BOOK PRIZES OF NOTE

The Man Booker Prize

ESTABLISHED: 1969

FOR: The best novel in English printed in the UK

PRIZE: £50,000

NOTABLE WINNERS: Iris Murdoch, *The Sea, the Sea* (1978); Salman Rushdie, *Midnight's Children* (1981); Kazuo Ishiguro, *The Remains of the Day* (1989); A.S. Byatt, *Possession* (1990); Hilary Mantel, *Wolf Hall* (2009) & *Bring up the Bodies* (2012)

Pulitzer Prize for Fiction

ESTABLISHED: 1917

FOR: Fiction by an American writer, preferably writing on American life

PRIZE: $10,000

NOTABLE WINNERS: Edith Wharton, *The Age of Innocence* (1921); Pearl S. Buck, *The Good Earth* (1932); Margaret Mitchell, *Gone with the Wind* (1937); Alice Walker, *The Color Purple* (1983); Donna Tartt, *The Goldfinch* (2014)

Women's Prize for Fiction[*]

ESTABLISHED: 1996

FOR: The best full-length novel by a woman written in English and published in the UK

---

[*] previously the Orange and then until 2017 the Baileys Prize.

PRIZE: £30,000 and a statue

NOTABLE WINNERS: Andrea Levy, *Small Island* (2004);
Lionel Shriver, *We Need to Talk About Kevin* (2005);
Chimamanda Ngozi Adichie, *Half of a Yellow Sun*
(2007); Ali Smith, *How to be Both* (2015)

COSTA BOOK OF THE YEAR*

ESTABLISHED: 1971

FOR: English-language book by writer from Britain
and Ireland

PRIZE: £30,000 (£5,000 for winning category
plus £25,000 for overall prize)

NOTABLE WINNERS: Philip Pullman, *The Amber
Spyglass* (2001); Mark Haddon, *The Curious Incident
of the Dog in the Night-time* (2003); Hilary Mantel,
Bring up the Bodies (2012)

SAMUEL JOHNSON PRIZE FOR NON-FICTION

ESTABLISHED: 1999

FOR: Best non-fiction writing in the English language

PRIZE: £25,000

NOTABLE WINNERS: Antony Beevor, *Stalingrad*
(1999); Kate Summerscale, *The Suspicions of Mr
Whicher* (2008); Helen Macdonald, *H is for Hawk*
(2014).

---

* formerly the Whitbread Prize.

THE TWENTY MOST INFLUENTIAL
ACADEMIC BOOKS OF ALL TIME

To celebrate National Academic Book Week in 2015 leading academic publishers, booksellers and librarians were asked to nominate the academic texts they felt had changed the world. From over 200 nominations a shortlist of twenty of the most influential academic books was produced:

A Brief History of Time by Stephen Hawking (1988)

A Vindication of the Rights of Woman
by Mary Wollstonecraft (1792)

Critique of Pure Reason by Immanuel Kant (1781)

Nineteen Eighty-Four by George Orwell (1949)

On the Origin of Species by Charles Darwin (1859)

Orientalism by Edward Said (1978)

Silent Spring by Rachel Carson (1962)

The Communist Manifesto by Karl Marx
and Friedrich Engels (1848)

The Complete Works of William Shakespeare
(c. 1590–c. 1613)

The Female Eunuch by Germaine Greer (1970)

The Making of the English Working Class
by E.P. Thompson (1963)

The Meaning of Relativity by Albert Einstein (1922)

The Naked Ape by Desmond Morris (1967)

The Prince by Niccolò Machiavelli (1532)

The Republic by Plato (380 BC)

The Rights of Man by Thomas Paine (1791)

The Second Sex by Simone de Beauvoir (1949)

The Uses of Literacy by Richard Hoggart (1957)

The Wealth of Nations by Adam Smith (1776)

Ways of Seeing by John Berger (1972)

It is interesting to note that, of the twenty books, over half (eleven) were published in the twentieth century – and nothing from the twenty-first century was included. Once the shortlist had been compiled, the public were then asked to vote to choose an overall winner. Charles Darwin's *On the Origin of Species*, first published in 1859, clinched the title.

BOOK PAPER

The paper used for books is traditionally off-white in colour to make the type easier to read, and must be opaque to prevent the text being seen through the page. Typically 60 to 90 g/m^2, book papers are fairly lightweight, ensuring a book does not become too bulky for binding.

Coated papers are generally used for illustrated books, children's books and graphic novels, whereas uncoated paper is used for traditional books. One of the highest quality book papers is Bible paper, so-called because it was used to print quality Bibles on. Bible paper is made from wood pulp combined with about 25 per cent linen or cotton rags – this makes the paper very strong, thin and lightweight, perfect for large, thick books such as encyclopedias and dictionaries.

Books account for less than one per cent of the world's timber usage (however, 40 per cent goes on making all types of paper including toilet roll, newspaper and office paper). Increasingly UK publishers are using paper from sustainable sources and with a high proportion of recycled material. Modern paper is made from chemical wood pulp which comes from both softwood and hardwood trees – there is no one tree that is most commonly used for making paper. The Forest Stewardship Council (FSC) ensures wood for paper is sourced from sustainable sources; their logo on a book means that the paper within does not use illegally logged timber.

THE BLOOMSBURY GROUP

The Bloomsbury Group were an informal set of writers, artists and intellectuals, many of whom had forged friendships while at Cambridge University through the Apostles (*see page 86*), who met regularly during the early part of the twentieth century to discuss and share ideas. So-called because they at first congregated and/or lived in the Bloomsbury area of London, the group most frequently met at the house of Clive and Vanessa Bell, both in Bloomsbury and at their country house, Charleston, in East Sussex.

In the post-Victorian world the group were seen as very liberal, even radical, with their left-wing views on sexuality, feminism and their anti-war stance challenging the accepted norms of the day.

Some of the key members of the group were:

Clive Bell (art critic) | Vanessa Bell (artist)
Virginia Woolf (writer) | Duncan Grant (artist)
Leonard Woolf (writer) | Roger Fry
(artist and critic) | Lytton Strachey (essayist)
John Maynard Keynes (economist)
E.M. Forster (writer)
Desmond MacCarthy (literary critic)

CHAPBOOKS

Chapbooks were cheap paper booklets sold by hawkers from the seventeenth century to the nineteenth. Chapbooks provided easily accessible reading material for children and the working classes and covered a wide variety of subjects such as sensationalist crime stories, poems, songs, biographies, almanacs, manuals, nursery rhymes and ghost stories.

Chapbooks were made from cheap, coarse paper folded many times to create a booklet, usually between eight and twenty-four pages long (although some are up to forty pages) and they often contained rough woodcuts as illustrations. Some chapbooks contained hand-coloured pictures, which might double their price. Hawkers, or 'chapmen', might sell their selection of chapbooks alongside other small essentials such as pins, seeds, gloves and spices.

Because of their flimsy nature chapbooks were fairly ephemeral and might be passed from person to person. However, today they are highly prized, as comparatively few survived and they provide a valuable glimpse into the popular culture of the day.

As printing processes advanced in the mid-nineteenth century, and methods of printing and distribution became cheaper, chapbooks fell out of fashion and their role as cheap disposable reading for children was taken on by 'penny dreadfuls' and, later, comics (*see page 114*). Today chapbooks are used as a format for creating short pamphlets of poetry which can be easily distributed and serve as a sample of the poet's work.

MILLS & BOON

Mills & Boon was established in 1908 by Gerald Mills and Charles Boon, initially as a general publisher. However, the first book the company published, in 1909, was the romance title *Arrows from the Dark* by Sophie Cole, the success of which paved the way for its future direction.

During the war years the escapism provided by romantic novels was especially welcome, and more and more of this genre aimed at women were published. Mills & Boon began using bright eye-catching book covers and placing large adverts in women's magazines and their brand began to grow. Romance titles were particularly popular in libraries. The company published new titles at a great rate, seeking out fresh new talent to keep the books coming and the appetite for romance stimulated.

By the 1960s Mills & Boon had started to produce paperbacks and standardized the length of their titles to between 188 and 192 pages. In 1971 they merged with Canadian publisher Harlequin and the brand expanded overseas, until by the mid-1980s they were selling 250 million books worldwide.[*]

---

[*] In 2003 over 2.5 million damaged or discontinued Mills & Boon titles were acquired by the construction firm building the M6 toll road. The books were pulped and poured onto the road as a strengthening and soundproofing layer before the asphalt was laid. Unbeknownst to most commuters on the M6 toll road, they are driving over approximately 45,000 old Mills & Boon titles per mile.

Today Mills & Boon publishes up to 120 new books every month and has developed a huge range of romance titles from historical bodice-rippers to supernatural love stories, ensuring there is a romance out there for everybody.

NOBEL PRIZE IN LITERATURE

The Nobel Prize in Literature is one of five prizes established by the 1895 will of inventor Alfred Nobel.[*] Since 1901 the Nobel Prize in Literature has been awarded 108 times to 112 different individuals (on four occasions the prize was shared by two people and seven times no prize was given, due to war).

The prize recognizes a writer's whole body of work rather than focusing on a particular book, and can be awarded to an author from anywhere in the world. Nobel Laureates receive a medal, a diploma with their citation on, and a large sum of money (the amount varies, but the Nobel Prize is the most valuable literary prize in the world).

Some notable winners of the prestigious prize are:

---

[*] Alfred Nobel invented dynamite. It is suggested that he was inspired to set up the Nobel prizes after a French newspaper wrongly printed an obituary about him titled 'The merchant of death is dead'. The obituary focused on his dynamite and munitions factories and it is thought Nobel was horrified that his legacy should be so negative. As a result Nobel left instructions in his will for the now world-famous prizes to be created, ensuring his name would forever be associated with great literature, scientific innovation and world peace.

1907	Rudyard Kipling (British)
1923	W.B. Yeats (Irish)
1925	George Bernard Shaw (Irish)
1932	John Galsworthy (British)
1936	Eugene O'Neill (American)
1938	Pearl S. Buck (American)
1948	T.S. Eliot (British)
1949	William Faulkner (American)
1953	Winston Churchill (British)
1954	Ernest Hemingway (American)
1957	Albert Camus (French)
1958	Boris Pasternak (Russian)
1962	John Steinbeck (American)
1964	Jean-Paul Sartre (French)
1969	Samuel Beckett (Irish)
1976	Saul Bellow (American)
1982	Gabriel García Márquez (Colombian)
1983	William Golding (British)
1993	Toni Morrison (American)
1995	Seamus Heaney (Irish)
1999	Günter Grass (German)
2003	J.M. Coetzee (South African)
2005	Harold Pinter (British)
2007	Doris Lessing (British)
2016	Bob Dylan (American)

France has had the most Nobel Prize in Literature laureates with 15, followed by the USA with 11 and the UK with 10. Of the 112 laureates to date, only 13 are women.

ODDEST TITLE OF THE YEAR

The Oddest Title of the Year Prize has been awarded every year since 1978.* Established by the Diagram Group as a humorous prize to celebrate the strangest book titles encountered at the Frankfurt Book Fair, since 1982 it has been overseen by Horace Bent, the diarist at trade publishing magazine *The Bookseller*. From 2000 the public have been allowed to vote on a selection of oddly titled books each year in order to select the worthy winner.†

Over the years some of the most notably odd titles to secure the prize have included:

Proceedings of the Second International
Workshop on Nude Mice (1978)
Oral Sadism and the Vegetarian Personality (1986)
American Bottom Archaeology (1993)
Developments in Dairy Cow Breeding:
New Opportunities to Widen the Use of Straw (1998)
The Big Book of Lesbian Horse Stories (2003)
Managing a Dental Practice: The Genghis Khan Way (2010)
How to Poo on a Date (2013)
Too Naked For the Nazis (2015)

---

* In a damning indictment of the imagination of the bookselling industry in both 1987 and 1991 no titles were deemed funny enough for the prize to be awarded.

† The prize has proved so popular with the public that in 2008 over 8,500 people voted on the Diagram Prize, compared to the 7,800 who voted for the Best of the Booker Prize.

COPYRIGHT TERMS
AROUND THE WORLD

The period of time for which a work remains in copyright varies considerably around the world, and is also subject to change.* For example:

UK	author's life plus 70 years
Australia	author's life plus 70 years
Canada	author's life plus 50 years
China	author's life plus 50 years
EU members	author's life plus 70 years†
India	author's life plus 60 years
Japan	author's life plus 50 years
Mexico	author's life plus 100 years
USA	author's life plus 70 years‡
Yemen	author's life plus 30 years

The Berne Convention is an international copyright agreement, created in 1886, which affords copyright protection of at least fifty years after the author's death in all countries signed up to the agreement. In addition, both the WIPO Copyright Treaty and the TRIPS Agreement of the WTO require compliance with the Berne Convention's minimum term.

---

* Expert advice should always be sought as to whether a work is in copyright.
† France, Ireland, Spain and the UK all have exceptions to this.
‡ Under certain circumstances this can be extended.

BOOK TOWNS

The concept of a book town was created in the 1960s when entrepreneur Richard Booth opened up a second-hand bookshop in the small market town of HAY-ON-WYE on the English/Welsh border. The bookshop proved extremely popular and before long had become one of the largest second-hand bookshops in Europe. Soon more bookshops opened and the local economy flourished as people flocked to the newly created book town. The status of Hay-on-Wye as the world's first and most important book town was cemented by the creation of its famous literary festival in 1987, which now tempts over 250,000 bookworms a year.

Since the success of Hay-on-Wye many other small towns or villages have attempted to revive their local economy by emulating the model. Some other notable book towns include:

REDU, BELGIUM   Redu is twinned with Hay-on-Wye. It opened its first bookshop in 1979 after villager Noel Anselot visited Hay and returned inspired. He wrote to local book dealers and asked them to come and set up bookshops in the original village buildings, such as barns, sheds and houses. Today there are seventeen second-hand book and comic shops and the village holds many literary events.

WIGTOWN, SCOTLAND   After the town's main local employers, a whisky distillery and creamery, shut down Wigtown was in danger of becoming run down. However, in 1998 salvation arrived in the shape of bookshops after Wigtown won a competition to become Scotland's only book town. Wigtown now has over twenty bookshops and a thriving literary festival.

HOBART, NEW YORK   This small book town in the Catskills has been attracting visitors to its six bookshops since 1999 and also hosts an annual Festival of Women Writers.

BREDEVOORT, NETHERLANDS   Bredevoort has over twenty second-hand and antiquarian bookshops and was designated a book town in 1993. Every third Saturday of the month this medieval town hosts a book market in the village square, which attracts book dealers from all over Europe.

INK

The first evidence of writing is from Sumer in Mesopotamia (modern-day Iraq) from 3,200 BC, but this did not involve ink; instead the letters were formed on clay tablets. Writing with ink evolved at roughly the same time in both China and Egypt in around 2,500 BC and went hand in hand with the development of papyrus (*see page* 7).

The first inks were created from a form of carbon called LAMPBLACK – so-called because in later times it was collected from the inside of oil lamps – which is formed by burning oily or resinous objects such as pine tree pitch or by burning oil with a wick. Lampblack is combined with glue or gum to form ink which is very stable and does not fade in the light, making it very durable.

In the fourth century BC in China a new ink was developed by blending lampblack, charred animal bones and animal glue to create a block; this could be dissolved in water when required. This style of ink came to be known as INDIA INK in the seventeenth century when Europeans began importing it from India. India ink was a long-lasting ink. However, it required absorbent paper to allow the ink to sink in and fix; thus on certain types of surface, such as non-absorbent parchment, the ink can dry and flake off.

By the eighth century AD a new type of ink was developed in Europe called IRON GALL INK. This was derived from iron salts and tannic acids from vegetables; its development complemented that of the quill pen (*see page 41*). Iron gall ink could be used on both vellum and parchment and so became the ink of choice in Europe from the twelfth to nineteenth centuries. Despite its popularity it does have the drawback that it can be corrosive and will eat through certain types of paper.

Woodblock printing developed in China in the second century AD; it was subsequently superseded by ceramic and then bronze moveable type in the twelfth century AD. Europe developed moveable type later, in the fifteenth century, independently of China, and Johannes Gutenberg (*see page 80*) designed a new style of ink with better adhesion to the metal type. This new ink was oil-based (rather than water-based), using a mixture of carbon, titanium, zinc and lead, with a texture that was more akin to varnish than to ink, and it was this that was used in the printing of the first books in Europe.

Today, following the developments in offset lithographic colour printing and inkjet printing, modern inks are numerous and complex. Inks have come a long way since they were mixed by hand: today the inks used in book production are formulated by chemists who blend pigments with a variety of chemicals for efficient printing and durability. However, most modern ink preparations are rather like a trademark and as such exact formulas remain secret.

A GLOSSARY OF
BOOK & MANUSCRIPT TERMS

ANTIQUARIAN BOOKS Books which are collectable, be they old, out of print or rare

APPENDIX Additional material relating to the work, generally found at the end of the book

BACKSTRIP The book spine's covering

BIFOLIUM Paper or parchment folded in half to create two leaves (or four pages)

BINDING The cover of the book over the book boards; might be leather, cloth or paper

BOOK BLOCK A book which has been printed, folded and sewn, but not yet bound

BOOK OF HOURS Popular medieval illuminated book used for private devotions, with list of prayers and scriptures to be read at prescribed canonical hours

BOOKPLATE A stick-in label which shows the ownership of the book

CODEX The earliest form of a book: quires of manuscript bound together to make a volume

COLOPHON Emblem, logo or note which identifies the publisher of the book (and in older books the publisher, date and place of printing), found on a page at the back of a book

CROWN The top edge of the spine

DUST JACKET Decorative paper wrapper to protect the binding of a book (*see page 87*)

E-BOOK Electronic book: a digital version of a book to be read on an e-reader (*see page 117*)

ENDPAPERS The first and last two pages of a book, one of which is pasted to the binding, the other left free

ERRATA Errors discovered in the book; publishers would often stick in a small erratum slip detailing these

FIRST EDITION The first printing of a book (*see page 58*)

FLYLEAF Blank pages at the end of the book

FLY TITLE Also known as half-title, a page before the title page which contains nothing but the title of the book

FOOT The bottom of the book's spine

FORE-EDGE The front edge of the text block, opposite the spine

FOXING Reddish brown (or fox-coloured) spotting and discolouration of the pages, found in nineteenth-century books due to the iron used in engravings

FRONTISPIECE An illustration at the start of the book, often facing the title page

FRONT MATTER The first few pages of a book, generally in this order: fly title, frontispiece, title page, imprint page, dedication, preface, table of contents, list of illustrations, introduction, acknowledgements, half-title

GALLEY PROOFS A proof of the running text

GUTTER The inner margins of a bound book

HALF BINDING A book which is bound in two separate materials; e.g. the spine and corners are bound in leather, the rest paper or cloth

HEADBAND A decorative, often coloured cloth, visible at the very top of the spine; in older books it forms part of the binding

ILLUMINATION Decoration applied by hand, frequently in gold or silver

IMPRINT Refers to the publisher or place of publication

INCUNABULE Book printed before 1501 (*see page 15*)

JUVENILIA Books or other compositions written when a writer was a child or teenager (*see page 91*)

K Stands for 'key', which is black in CMYK colour printing (C is cyan, M is magenta, Y is yellow)

LEAF A single thickness of paper; each leaf has two printed sides

LIMITED EDITION A book which is deliberately printed in small numbers, often signed by author or illustrator, to make it special

MANUSCRIPT The original text produced by the author – handwritten, typed or digital; also handwritten texts created by scribes

MARGIN The space surrounding the text on each page

MARGINALIA Notes or diagrams written in the margins by previous users/owners of the book

MOROCCO Leather, usually made from goatskin, used in book binding

NOTCH BINDING A method of perfect binding: as the pages are gathered, notches are cut along the spine and hot glue used to hold them together

OCTAVO The most common size for modern hardback books (approximately 5 inches by 8 inches); to make the book the paper is folded to create eight leaves or sixteen pages

OUT OF PRINT Any book which is no longer in print, and the available numbers of which are therefore limited

PERFECT BINDING A method of binding paperback books whereby the pages are glued together at the spine before being placed in the cover

PLATES Whole-page illustrations which are printed separately from the text

PROOFS Versions of the book produced prior to publication, often uncorrected, to check printing and to send out to reviewers

QUARTER BINDING A book whose spine is bound in a different material to the rest of the book

QUIRE A group of pages created by folding a single sheet, which are then gathered together to be sewn or glued into a book

RECTO The right-hand page of an opened book (the front of a leaf)

SIGNATURE The letters/numbers printed at the bottom of the first leaf (and sometimes every leaf in the first half) as a guide to the binder when assembling the quires; this has also come to mean gathering

SLIPCASE A cardboard case which might be covered in paper, leather or cloth and holds a book or series of books with the spines facing out

SPINE The backbone of the book

TEXT BLOCK The main body of the book with the covers and bindings removed

TITLE PAGE In modern books contains all the information needed to catalogue the book – title, subtitle, author or editor, publisher etc.

TOOLING The decoration of leather bindings using heated tools to impress a design

TOP EDGE GILT (TEG) When the topmost edges of the pages have been covered in gold leaf or gilt

UNOPENED A book where the pages of the quires have yet to be cut open, a process which was usually completed by the binder

VERSO The left-hand page of an opened book (the back of a leaf)

WATERMARK Faint design created in the paper during manufacture and visible when held up to the light; usually identifies the maker

WOODCUT Early form of printing illustrations carved out from a wood block

WORMHOLES Holes in books made by bookworms

JOHANNES GUTENBERG

Surprisingly little is known about Johannes Gutenberg,[*] the man who developed the modern printing press in Europe, and yet his invention was to revolutionize book printing and as a result bring books to the masses. It is thought Gutenberg was born around the very end of the fourteenth century in Mainz, Germany. From legal records we know that he initially worked crafting metal hand mirrors which were used by pilgrims when visiting holy sites. It is unclear how he went from mirrors to moveable type but clearly his metalworking skills were strong. He must have had a clear vision of what he wanted to achieve as it is thought that it took him at least ten years to develop his moveable type. To finance his work Gutenberg borrowed money from Johann Fust, but the two later fell out and a court ordered Gutenberg to return the money with interest and hand over some of his printing equipment, a move that would much benefit Fust.

In *c.* 1455 Johannes Gutenberg printed the first substantial book in Europe, the famous *Gutenberg Bible* (*see page 44*). Approximately 180 copies of the Bible were printed, some on paper and some on vellum. Today only 49 (twelve of which are on vellum) copies survive, making it one of the most valuable books

---

* So mysterious a figure is Gutenberg that even the engravings we have of him were produced many years after his death and so provide just an approximation of his appearance.

in the world. Contemporary evidence from a letter written by the future Pope Pius II to Cardinal Carvajal suggests that the quality of the Bibles caused amazement, with Pius commenting that you could even read the text without glasses, indicating that the clarity was a huge technological leap. Despite their high price tag of 30 florins, all the Bibles were sold before they had all been printed, proving that printing was a good business opportunity.

It is unclear what happened to Gutenberg in his later life but it is known that the Archbishop of Mainz provided him with a pension and that he died in *c.* 1468. Johann Fust continued in the printing business (with the equipment Gutenberg had been forced to hand over to him) with Gutenberg's assistant Peter Schöffer, and together they created the first book in Europe to contain the names of the printers, a beautifully crafted psalter which was printed in 1457. Within twenty-five years of the first printing of the Gutenberg Bible, the printing press had spread around Europe and workshops had been established in many leading cities, heralding the advent of cheaper printing and the democratization of knowledge.

Tantalisingly we know of a number of books, poems and plays written by esteemed authors that have been lost, whether by accident or design. Below is a summary of some lost works of note:

CARDENIO BY WILLIAM SHAKESPEARE   Evidence suggests that Shakespeare's company the King's Men performed a play of this title for King James I in 1613 and that the play was co-authored by Shakespeare and John Fletcher (his collaborator on *Henry VIII* and *Two Noble Kinsmen*). It is posited that the play may have been inspired by *Don Quixote* (which was translated into English in 1612) as a character named Cardenio features in the Spanish masterpiece. The original play may never be found but in the eighteenth century Shakespeare scholar Lewis Theobald claimed to have discovered the manuscript* and published it with his own 'improvements' as *The Double Falsehood*. Modern scholars have analysed this text and suggest that it may indeed have been based upon Shakespeare's original lost text.

MARGITES BY HOMER   The text of Homer's comic epic poem, composed in *c.* 700 BC, has been lost but we know of its existence from other writers. Notably

---

* The manuscript was supposedly stored at the Covent Garden Playhouse, which unfortunately burned down in 1808, so we may never know if it was truly the lost play.

Aristotle praised the comedic brilliance of the poem. Small fragments of the poem survive. It is known that the poem concerned the character of Margite, who was so stupid he did not know which parent gave birth to him.

A Brilliant Career by James Joyce   In 1900 Joyce sent this play to William Archer, a Scottish drama critic and translator of Henrik Ibsen. Archer replied with mostly positive comments; however, for some reason Joyce decided the work was no good and destroyed the manuscript in 1902. All that remains is the title page, which contains Joyce's dedication 'To My own Soul I dedicate the first true work of my life'.

A World War I novel by Ernest Hemingway The young Ernest Hemingway wrote a novel about his experiences during the First World War. It was bundled up with various other short stories and notes and packed into a suitcase. In 1922, Hemingway's first wife, Hadley, took the suitcase on a train from Paris to Lausanne in Switzerland, where she was meeting Ernest, who was covering the European Peace Conference there for the *Toronto Daily Star*. Hemingway hoped to show his work to an editor named Lincoln Steffens, who had shown an interest in his ideas. Unfortunately at some point on the journey the suitcase was stolen and the manuscripts lost forever. Hemingway was said to have been very upset by the loss, but refused to attempt to rewrite the lost novel, leaving its contents unknown to the public.

INVENTIO FORTUNATA   In the thirteenth century an unknown English monk travelled to the Arctic Circle and recorded his impressions of the forbidding landscape, including a description of what he claimed was the North Pole. This work was published as *Inventio Fortunata* (or *The Discovery of the Fortunate Islands*) and supposedly gifted to Edward III in *c.* 1360. The book went missing but not before its contents had been described to Flemish writer Jacobus Cnoyen, who included a summary of it in his work *Itinerarium*. Unfortunately this book is also lost to history. However, celebrated cartographer Gerard Mercator wrote to English magician and astronomer John Dee in 1577 with a description of the North Pole taken directly from *Itinerarium*, and it is thought that when he published his famous 1595 map of the world it was this very description he used to inform his depiction of the North Pole.

AMONG THE PROPHETS BY GEORGE GISSING   The Victorian novelist George Gissing is perhaps best known for his novel *New Grub Street* (1891). Despite being a prolific writer he did not always have confidence in his work. In the 1900s, towards the end of his writing career (and life), he wrote a novel titled *Among the Prophets* which was said to concern spiritual enlightenment. It is thought he completed the work but ultimately felt unsatisfied with it and so had his agent burn all copies.

ISLE OF THE CROSS BY HERMAN MELVILLE   This lost novel would have been Melville's eighth work.

However, his publisher Harper & Brothers rejected it. The novel was inspired by the true story of Agatha Hatch, who had rescued a shipwrecked man; he recovered and married her, only later to abandon her. The manuscript has never been found. It is supposed that it was rejected due to fears that the book could be seen as libellous were readers to recognize the real characters.

THE POOR MAN AND THE LADY BY THOMAS HARDY   This was the first novel written by Thomas Hardy in 1867. He sent it to numerous publishers but it was rejected by all, so Hardy moved on to other works. The book was about the romance between the son of a peasant and the daughter of a squire and was fairly strong in its negative depiction of the establishment. It was this that prevented the book from being published as, although most publishers recognized its literary merit, the subject was something of a hot potato at that time. Unfortunately Hardy destroyed the manuscript, so the only hints we have as to its contents were later works, thought to be based on his first novel, such as *Desperate Remedies* and the poem 'A Poor Man and a Lady'.

THE APOSTLES

The Apostles is a secret Cambridge University society, founded in 1820 by George Tomlinson, future Bishop of Gibraltar. Also known as the Cambridge Conversazione Society, it became known as the Apostles as its original group had twelve members. Ostensibly a debating club, the society would meet to discuss such big questions as religion, truth and ethics. The Apostles has become well known for including many Cambridge students who went on to become literary greats. Indeed the germ of the Bloomsbury Group (*see page 64*) was sown in the Apostles. Most Apostles come from Trinity, St Johns and King's colleges and one cannot simply join but must be nominated and approved by current members. It was only in 1970 that women were allowed to join. Since the society's inception all the names of the members have been noted down in a leather-bound notebook, along with some of the issues they have debated. This book is considered a great treasure of the society. The following literary figures were all members of this august society:

Lytton Strachey | Leonard Woolf
Rupert Brooke | E.M. Forster | Arthur Hallam
Richard Moncton Milnes | Alfred, Lord Tennyson

DUST JACKETS

The first paper dust jackets were introduced in the nineteenth century. Initially they were just plain paper wraps, designed to protect fine bindings from damage when they were transported from the bookbinder to the library. These plain jackets were intended to be discarded once the book had safely reached its destination. Sometimes dust jackets were produced with windows that allowed the fine decorative bindings beneath to be seen; this soon developed into the jackets themselves including decoration. Due to their ephemeral nature not many early dust jackets survive; indeed, in the special collection of dust jackets held by the British Library* the earliest example is from the relatively late date of 1919. In 2009 a librarian at the Bodleian Library in Oxford rediscovered the earliest known dust jacket. The white paper covering, which dates from 1830, was designed to fully wrap around a silk-covered gift book titled *Friendship's Offering*. Traces of sealing wax revealed that the wrapper completely enclosed the book.

By the 1920s publishers had realized the promotional potential of the highly decorative dust jacket – not only would they catch a reader's eye but they also had space to advertise other titles available from the publisher. This period also saw the rise of the book

---

* The collection, which includes over 11,000 dust jackets, is at the time of writing on loan to the Victoria and Albert Museum.

'blurb' – a promotional summary of the book and perhaps a short biography of its author that appeared, generally, on the back cover of the dust jacket. Dust jackets had become a new way to draw in a reader, and so the designs became more eye-catching.

Surviving dust jackets from the 1920s are still very sought after as they were easily lost or damaged. One of the most iconic and valuable dust jackets is that for the first edition of *The Great Gatsby* by F. Scott Fitzgerald. The jacket, produced in 1925, was one of the first to use a strikingly designed image (by little-known Spanish artist Francis Cugat) – an intense blue background with two eyes looking out over the lights of Coney Island. Such is the value of this dust jacket that, whereas a first edition is valued at around £5,000, one with a complete dust jacket could sell for as much as £120,000. Thus book jackets have developed from a simple way to protect a fine binding to collectable pieces of art in their own right.

MEDIEVAL ILLUMINATED MANUSCRIPTS

Early manuscripts were written by hand by scribes, and some were beautifully and meticulously decorated with illuminated illustrations. Illuminations (from the Latin *illuminare*, to light up) are embellished illustrations often using luminous colours and gold or silver leaf. They might appear as decorated borders, small illustrations or illuminated letters and were nearly always embellishments in religious texts. Larger illuminated pictures not integrated into the text which took up a half or full page were known as miniatures. Although some Egyptian manuscripts used illuminations, such as the *Book of the Dead* from the twentieth century BC, the first known illuminated manuscript from Western Christianity was the Quedlinburg fragment, which was produced in the fourth century AD. The production of illuminated manuscripts in Europe took off around the sixth century AD and lasted until the birth of modern printing techniques in the fifteenth century signalled its demise. Depending on the geographical location or time period, different elements were used in decoration. Most scribes mixed their own pigments.* Below is a summary of some of the many minerals and pigments used in medieval illuminations:

KERMES   A natural red pigment created by crushing the female *Kermes vermilio*, a shield louse which is found across the Mediterranean region on kermes oaks. The word *kermes* is said to be the origin of the English word 'crimson'.

LEAD WHITE   This pigment was created by sealing strips of lead above urine or vinegar and then burying it in a dung heap for a few days. A crust would form on the lead, which was scraped off and crushed to make lead white. Widely used in illumination, it was also used

---

* Pigments were mixed with binding agents – substances ranging from egg tempera to earwax – to make the colour easier to apply.

as a cosmetic to whiten women's faces – an inadvisable practice as the lead content rendered it poisonous.

SAFFRON YELLOW   Made by collecting and crushing the stigmas of crocus plants, saffron yellow would sometimes be used as a substitute for gold leaf.

TERRE VERTE   Terre verte or green earth was one of the earliest pigments used in illuminations. It is derived from the minerals celadonite and glauconite. Green earth is a muted yellowish green to grey-green and was generally used as an undertone for flesh tones.

ULTRAMARINE   This bright blue colour was the most expensive pigment used during the Middle Ages, more costly even than gold. It is a natural pigment created by crushing the semi-precious stone lapis lazuli, which was sourced from mines in Afghanistan. Due to its cost and scarcity, ultramarine was often reserved for colouring the bright blue cloaks worn by Jesus or the Virgin Mary.

VERDIGRIS   Created when plates of copper are painted with vinegar (or acetic acid), causing a reaction with the copper; a crust is formed, which is scraped off and used to create a blue-green pigment. However, the copper is corrosive to parchment and as it ages the colour can turn from green to brown or black.

VERMILION   Derived from the mineral cinnabar it creates a red colour, ranging from orange-red through to a darker blue-red. Cinnabar is a toxic mercury sulphide, so mining it is very dangerous. Despite this, such was its bright red hue that it was much in demand.

WOAD   Traditionally used in Europe to create a blue colour (it is said to have been the pigment used by early Britons to dye their skin blue). It is extracted from the leaves of the plant *Isatis tinctoria*. Woad was extensively utilized in medieval manuscripts – it was used to create the blue colours used in the Lindisfarne Gospels. From the sixteenth century, as trade with India grew, woad was replaced with the more intense blue of indigo.

JUVENILIA

A writer's juvenilia are their early works, written when they were still a child or young adult. In most cases these writings are released retrospectively after an adult writer has gained some repute, as a way to mark their creative progress. However, some juvenilia have been published when the writer was in their youth and only became labelled as such posthumously. Below are some juvenilia of note:

THE BRONTË SIBLINGS   Probably some of the most famous juvenilia are that by the Brontë siblings. Charlotte, Emily, Anne and their brother Branwell created the fictional worlds of Glass Town, Angria and Gondal, and the fledgling writers wrote tiny books filled with histories of these invented worlds. Although no great literary merit exists in these childish books, they offer scholars a fascinating insight into the development and character of the Brontë siblings. Only around twenty examples of Brontë juvenilia survives, nine of which are at Harvard Library and others at the Brontë Museum and the British Library.

JANE AUSTEN   Three volumes of stories, poems and sketches survive from Jane Austen's childhood, written between the ages of 10 and 17. The writings were clearly written to be read and shared among family and friends, and the notebooks show a fair amount of wear, suggesting they were indeed enjoyed by many. Different in style from Austen's adult novels, these childish works are exaggerated and exuberant. The first volume is held at the Bodleian Library in Oxford (MS. Don. e. 7), the other two at the British Library.

ALFRED, LORD TENNYSON   In 1827 when the 18-year-old Tennyson went up to Trinity College in Cambridge, he and his brother Charles published a collection of poetry *Poems by Two Brothers*. At the time this was not labelled juvenilia, but as Tennyson went on to later great success his early works were relabelled such to differentiate them from his more famous mature works.

ROBERT LOUIS STEVENSON   Stevenson was a sickly child and found solace in writing, especially in creating fictional travelogues. Many of his childish works survive, some from when he was just 6 years old, including *The History of Moses*, dictated to his mother and illustrated by himself, which is held at the National Library of Scotland.

JOHN RUSKIN   Victorian art critic John Ruskin showed precocious writing talent as a child, composing pages of poetry at the age of 10, which his devout mother Margaret thoroughly disapproved of. Ruskin himself published his works of juvenilia, remarking that they showed his lifelong consistency of thought.

CHARLES DICKENS   Only in recent years have some fragments of Charles Dickens's juvenilia come to light. In 2012 they were published together in a short book for the first time, entitled *The Bill of Fare, O'Thello & Other Early Works*.

SOME QUOTATIONS ON BOOKS AND READING

'Clearly one must read every good book
at least once every ten years.'
C.S. Lewis (1898–1963)

'When I get a little money, I buy books.
If any is left, I buy food and clothes.'
Erasmus (1466–1536)

'There is no friend as loyal as a book.'
Ernest Hemingway (1899–1961)

'A book must be an ice-axe
to break the seas frozen inside our soul.'
Franz Kafka (1883–1924)

'To learn to read is to light a fire;
every syllable that is spelled out is a spark.'
Victor Hugo (1802–1885)

'Books are the best of things, well used;
abused, among the worst.'
Ralph Waldo Emerson (1803–1882)

'To acquire the habit of reading is to construct for
yourself a refuge from almost all the miseries of life.'
W. Somerset Maugham (1874–1965)

'Of all the things which man can do or make here
below, by far the most momentous, wonderful, and
worthy are the things we call books.'
Thomas Carlyle (1795–1881)

'Not all readers are leaders,
but all leaders are readers.'
Harry S. Truman (1884–1972)

'A writer only begins a book. A reader finishes it.'
Samuel Johnson (1709–1784)

LEGAL DEPOSIT

The concept of legal deposit, according to which a copy of every book published in the country is preserved in a national library, was developed by Sir Thomas Bodley, founder of Oxford's Bodleian Library. In 1610, Bodley reached an agreement with the Stationers' Company of London that a copy of every book published in England would be deposited at his library. This agreement was the forerunner of legal deposit, which came into force in 1662, whereby printers were obliged to supply the libraries of Oxford and Cambridge, in addition to the Royal Library (now the British Library), with three copies of every book published in the UK.* Legal deposit ensures that national collections are constantly growing and represent and preserve the output of the British publishing industry. Legal deposit was further reiterated under the first Copyright Act of 1709 and again in 1911. In 2003 and 2013 legal deposit was extended to include online and digital items such as websites, blogs, CD-ROMs and social media, ensuring libraries keep apace with technological innovation.

The following libraries (with date they joined in parentheses) are the six legal deposit libraries in the UK:

---

* The British Library is the only library which automatically receives a copy of *every* book published in the UK or Ireland; the other libraries are entitled to *request* any book published within the previous twelve months.

Bodleian Library, Oxford (1662)
Cambridge University Library (1662)
The British Library (1709)
National Library of Scotland
(previously Advocates Library) (1709)
Trinity College Library, Dublin (1801)
National Library of Wales (1911)

BOOKPLATES

Bookplates are small printed labels which are pasted into a book to indicate ownership. They are also known as *ex libris* as many are adorned with the Latin term, meaning 'from the library of', allowing collectors to trace the ownership of a book. Bookplates can be plain and simple or elaborately embellished; sometimes they feature a motif, motto or coat of arms to represent the book's owner.

The earliest bookplates are from fifteenth-century Germany. During this period books were rare and expensive items; consequently book owners were keen to ensure their precious works were clearly labelled with ownership.

Over the years many famous artists have designed bookplates, making them desirable and collectable items in and of themselves. Aubrey Beardsley, Marc Chagall, Kate Greenaway, Albrecht Dürer, William Hogarth and Rockwell Kent all created bookplates over the years, contributing to an art form which by the nineteenth century had become very collectable. Numerous notable people had their own bookplate designs, including Queen Victoria, Jack London, George Washington, Lord Byron and Charles Dickens.

From the mid-twentieth century, as books became cheaper to make and buy, bookplates became less vital and fell out of fashion. However, historical bookplates remain important, not just as tiny works of art but for librarians and collectors – the bookplates allow individual collections which make up the whole to remain visible, aiding librarians in tracing the ownership and provenance of an individual item.

THE WORLD'S LARGEST BOOKSHOP

The official largest bookshop in the world (according to the *Guinness Book of Records*) is Barnes & Noble at 105 5th Avenue, New York. The store is 154,250 square feet in size and boasts 12.87 miles of shelving. However, because Barnes & Noble also offers a lot of non-book stock in its store another bookshop is claiming the title. Powell's City of Books bookstore in Portland, Oregon, claims to be the world's largest independent used and new bookstore in the world, containing over 1 million books in 3,500 different sections.

POETS LAUREATE

The post of British Poet Laureate originated in 1616 when King James I provided the writer Ben Jonson with a pension, setting a precedent for a court-supported writer. The first official Poet Laureate was John Dryden, appointed by warrant by Charles II in 1668.* It was Thomas Shadwell, appointed in 1689, who started the tradition of releasing a poem to celebrate the monarch's birthday and another to celebrate the New Year.

Alfred, Lord Tennyson was probably the most famous and beloved laureate, composing 'The Charge of the Light Brigade' during his tenure. Such was the respect for Tennyson that the post of laureate was kept vacant for four years following his death. Today the role is held for a set term of ten years and is honorary, meaning the poet may choose what to write about and when they release their poems. Some notable Poets Laureate are:

John Dryden (1668–69)
Colley Cibber (1730–57)
William Wordsworth (1843–50)
Alfred, Lord Tennyson (1850–92)

---

* Unfortunately for Dryden he managed to be both the first poet laureate and the first to be dismissed from the post. In 1688 when the Protestant William III and Mary II ascended to the throne Catholic-convert Dryden refused to swear an oath of allegiance to the new monarchs and so was replaced by Thomas Shadwell.

Cecil Day-Lewis (1968–72)
John Betjeman (1972–84)
Ted Hughes (1984–98)
Andrew Motion (1999–2009)
Carol Ann Duffy (2009–)

Three poets are known to have turned down the laureateship: Thomas Gray in 1757 (seemingly due to a lack of self-confidence), Samuel Rogers in 1850 (due to his advanced years) and Walter Scott in 1813, who recommended Robert Southey instead.

BOOKS PRINTED WITH MISTAKES

In the world of book collecting, those which were printed with errors or mistakes can become highly sought after. It might be because the inclusion of the error indicates that it is an early printing of a book or because once the misprint had been noticed the books were recalled and pulped, making them scarce. Some famous printing errors are:

THE WICKED BIBLE   Printed in 1631 this edition of the King James Bible had a rather crucial error in its printing of the Ten Commandments. 'Thou shalt not commit adultery' was rendered as 'Thou shalt commit adultery', much to the delight of sinners everywhere. It is thought that only ten copies survive, making the edition now extremely valuable.

THE ADVENTURES OF HUCKLEBERRY FINN Mark Twain's celebrated novel was first published in America in 1885 and contained a couple of errors, including on page 57, 'with the was' instead of 'with the saw.' This error was corrected in the second printing. The presence of the typo therefore indicates a true first edition.

THE SUN ALSO RISES The first edition of *The Sun Also Rises* (1926) by Ernest Hemingway was printed with an error on page 181, line 26. Instead of 'stopped' it was printed with an extra p as 'stoppped'. The dust jacket also listed his previous work as 'In Our Times' instead of 'In Our Time'. These errors in a first edition make it far more valuable than the corrected second printing of the book.

AN AMERICAN TRAGEDY The first edition of Theodore Dreiser's 1925 novel *An American Tragedy* was printed with a rather amusing typo. Instead of the word 'ships' the edition was printed with: 'like two small chips being tossed about on a rough but friendly sea.' — creating a rather glorious, yet erroneous, mental image.

THE PRISONER OF AZKABAN The first British edition of *The Prisoner of Azkaban* by J.K. Rowling, the third book of the Harry Potter series, was printed with an error. The imprint page, instead of listing J.K. Rowling, the author's pen name, was printed with the author's real name, Joanne Rowling. The second printing was corrected and so a book with this error indicates a true first edition and is thus more valuable.

THE TIME MACHINE   When H.G. Wells's seminal novel was published in America in 1895, publisher Holt accidentally printed the title page with the wrong initial: H.S. Wells. This first edition is also especially valuable, as the English edition published in the same year by Heinemann contained sixteen chapters and an epilogue (comprising additional material taken from earlier serialized versions of the story), whereas the Holt version contained just twelve. Most versions today are therefore based on the longer Heinemann edition.

THE HISTORY OF PAPER

The word 'paper' derives from papyrus (*see page 7*), the plant used by ancient Egyptians to create thin sheets on which to write. Although papyrus is similar to paper, the method by which it is created, by layering reeds, does not fit the definition of paper as being made from macerated fibres, and therefore true papermaking is credited to the Chinese in *c.* 100 AD. The traditional tale tells that the invention of paper occurred in 105 AD, when the chief eunuch of the Han Chinese Emperor Ho-Ti, T'sai-Lun, developed a technique to macerate plant fibres. The fibres (derived from mulberry, hemp, cloth, bark and grass) were placed in a vat of water and a screen was submerged in the vat until it caught the fibres on its surface. The screen would then be removed from the water and left to dry, creating a thin layer of dried plant fibres – the precursor to all modern paper. Such was the importance of this discovery that T'sai-Lun was deified as the god of papermaking.

The techniques of papermaking stayed in China for hundreds of years as a closely guarded secret until the seventh century, when it spread to Japan. By this time paper was being made from hemp rags, rice or tea straw and bamboo. In 751 AD a Chinese caravan was captured near Samarkand in modern-day Uzbekistan. Among the prisoners were several master papermakers, who were soon put to work creating paper in Samarkand, which became a new centre for papermaking. From here the craft slowly spread through central Asia, and from the ninth century into the Middle East.

Paper from Asia and the Islamic world began to appear in Europe in the eleventh century and a paper mill was established in Toledo in 1065, starting a steady march across Europe, with a mill appearing in France in 1190; in Fabriano, Italy, in 1276; in Mainz, Germany, in 1320; and in Britain in 1490. When the first substantial printed book, the Gutenberg Bible, came off the printing press in Germany in 1455 it was printed on vellum and paper. Early European paper pulp was made from recycled rags of linen and cotton, and before the discovery of chlorine in the eighteenth century was unbleached, and thus frequently had a greyish hue. Watermarks in the paper to show where it was produced first appeared in Fabriano in 1282 and soon became commonplace.

There was a huge demand for paper as books became more affordable, but as European paper was made from rags there was not always enough fibre to keep up with demand. More and more paper mills began producing paper but it was still a highly skilled task, with each sheet fashioned by hand. A number of early papermaking machines were designed, by far the most successful of which was the Fourdrinier machine patented in France in 1807. The steam-powered machine enabled a continuous process for making paper, with pulp constantly fed onto a moving mesh belt, greatly speeding up production. Wood pulp was finally discovered as a cheap and plentiful source of paper in 1843. Coupled with improvements in automated papermaking machines, this rendered paper ever more abundant and affordable.

WORLD BOOK DAY

World Book Day was established by UNESCO and first celebrated on 23 April 1995. The event is now celebrated all over the world every year on 23 April, a date chosen because it is the date of death for notable writers William Shakespeare, Miguel Cervantes and Inca Garcilaso de la Vega. In the UK and Ireland, World Book Day is held, exceptionally, on the first Thursday in March because 23 April is already cel-ebrated as St George's Day. World Book Day was created to promote books and reading globally and to recognize the many wonderful writers. In Britain, World Book Day is probably best known as a day many parents dread as they are forced to source a costume for the school's 'dress up as your favourite book character' day. Additionally since 1994 Britain has celebrated National Poetry Day every October, promoting poetry with events, readings and other poetical acts.

TRANSLATED BOOKS

According to UNESCO's *Index Translationum*, which has been tracking translated books since 1979, the top ten most common original languages for translated works are:

RANK	LANGUAGE	NO. OF TITLES
1.	English	1,265,324
2.	French	225,799
3.	German	208,091
4.	Russian	103,599
5.	Italian	69,544
6.	Spanish	54,554
7.	Swedish	39,977
8.	Japanese	29,242
9.	Danish	21,250
10.	Latin	19,952

It is interesting to note that the language into which most books are translated is German, followed by French, Spanish, English and then Japanese.

The most translated book in the world is the Bible, which has had its entirety or portions of it translated into 2,883 different languages (out of approximately 7,000 known languages in the world).

KURT VONNEGUT'S TIPS ON WRITING A SHORT STORY

In the introduction to Kurt Vonnegut's short story collection *Bagombo Snuff Box* (1999), the writer included a series of tips on how to write a good short story:

- ☞ Use the time of a total stranger in such a way that he or she will not feel the time was wasted.
- ☞ Give the reader at least one character he or she can root for.
- ☞ Every character should want something, even if it is only a glass of water.
- ☞ Every sentence must do one of two things – reveal character or advance the action.
- ☞ Start as close to the end as possible.
- ☞ Be a sadist. No matter how sweet and innocent your leading characters, make awful things happen to them – in order that the reader may see what they are made of.

- ☞ Write to please just one person. If you open a window and make love to the world, so to speak, your story will get pneumonia.
- ☞ Give your readers as much information as possible as soon as possible. To heck with suspense. Readers should have such complete understanding of what is going on, where and why, that they could finish the story themselves, should cockroaches eat the last few pages.

OLDEST DEBUT NOVELISTS

An old adage has it that 'good things come to those who wait'. This could perhaps be said to be true of the following authors, who all had their first book published after their fortieth birthday:

WRITER	TITLE	AGE
William S. Burroughs	*Junkie* (1953)	40
George Eliot	*Adam Bede* (1859)	40
Arthur Miller	*Tropic of Cancer* (1934)	44
Marquis de Sade	*Justine* (1791)	51
Richard Adams	*Watership Down* (1972)	52
Anna Sewell	*Black Beauty* (1877)	57
Laura Ingalls Wilder	*Little House in the Big Woods* (1932)	65
Frank McCourt	*Angela's Ashes* (1996)	66

Also of note is Doris Lessing, who had a long and fruitful career, publishing dozens of novels, essays and poems. Her first, *The Grass is Singing* (1950), was published when she was 31 and her last, *Alfred and Emily* (2008), when she was 89.

BOOKBINDING

The art of bookbinding began in the first century AD as the first codices developed; before this most writing was on clay tablets or scrolls (*see page 7*). Codices (*see page 125*) were made from leaves of vellum or parchment sewn together between two boards – the recognizable shape of a modern book. This development not only made the book stronger but also made it easier to store, and this method slowly became established as the norm.

During the early medieval period most books were religious texts, produced by hand in monasteries; each volume would take many months of meticulous work to create. Early bindings, sometimes known as 'supported sewing', were created by sewing through the text block onto flexible bands or cords, held across the spine at right angles. These would then be kept flat by holding them together between wooden boards. As the art of binding developed these boards were joined to the rest of the book by wrapping leather around them, and by *c.* 400 AD the leather was being decorated with tooling.

The oldest intact surviving European book is the St Cuthbert Gospel, which was beautifully bound in embossed tooled leather and buried with St Cuthbert c. 698 in Lindisfarne, Northumberland. The book was retrieved from Cuthbert's coffin in 1104; since 2012 it has been held at the British Library.

For hundreds of years bookbinding showed little change as monks continued to oversee the majority of book production. However, with the advent of paper and the printing press, books moved out of the monastery and into the mainstream. This development meant that suddenly many more books were being produced, and so more efficient methods to create bindings were needed. Sewing techniques became more streamlined, with text blocks sewn into recessed cords. Pasteboards – layers of paper laminated together using pressure – started to be used to cover the books instead of wood, which meant specialist woodworking was no longer required and holes could be more easily be punched by hand into the pasteboards.

The sixteenth century saw books becoming smaller and thus easier to bind. Tanned goatskin, also known as Morocco, was introduced into Europe as a book covering. Ornate gold-embossed bindings came into fashion from the fifteenth century and titles began to migrate to the spine. Most books were bought from the printer without a binding and many collectors would have all their books bound in a similar style to create a beautiful library.

By the late nineteenth century bookbinding took another leap forward as machines were developed to sew, glue, trim and cover books. By the 1930s, with the advent of paperback books (*see page 55*), perfect binding – whereby books were glued rather than sewn together – had become the norm.

TRADITIONAL BOOK SIZES

Traditionally book sizes are described by envisaging the size of the page as a fraction of the large sheet on which it was originally printed. When printing a book an even number of pages are printed on both sides of a large piece of paper; this paper is then folded and the edges cut so that the pages are in the correct order. The names of book sizes are based on the original paper and the fractional size of the page; for example, a royal octavo would be a page one-eighth of the size of a royal sheet of paper. The most common traditional paper names and sizes (sheet sizes vary by country) are as follows:

royal 20 × 25 inches
medium 18 × 23 inches
crown 15 × 19 inches

The exact page measurements differ slightly depending on the binding and trimming. A table of traditional book sizes follows:

name	times folded	leaves per sheet	pages per sheet	page size (inches)
royal folio	1	2	4	20 × 12½
royal quarto	2	4	8	12½ × 10
royal octavo	3	8	16	10 × 6¼
royal 16mo	4	16	32	6¼ × 5
royal 32mo	5	32	64	5 × 3⅛
royal 64mo	6	64	128	3⅛ × 2½
medium folio	1	2	4	18 × 11½
medium quarto	2	4	8	11½ × 9
medium octavo	3	8	16	9 × 5¾
medium 16mo	4	16	32	5¾ × 4½
medium 32mo	5	32	64	4½ × 2⅞
medium 64mo	6	64	128	2⅞ × 2¼
crown folio	1	2	4	15 × 10
crown quarto	2	4	8	10 × 7½
crown octavo	3	8	16	7½ × 5
crown 16mo	4	16	32	5 × 3¾
crown 32mo	5	32	64	3¾ × 2½
crown 64mo	6	64	128	2½ × 1⅞

Additionally there are classifications for oversize books, such as the elephant folio, which is up to 23 inches high; atlas folio, which is up to 25 inches high; and the largest book size, double elephant, which is used for books up to 50 inches high.

THE WORLD'S MOST MYSTERIOUS
BOOK: THE VOYNICH MANUSCRIPT

In 1912 a Polish-American bookseller, Wilfrid M. Voynich, bought a number of texts from a Jesuit college near Rome. One of the books immediately caught his attention as it was seemingly very old and yet written in some unknown script and was full of illustrations of plants, people and constellations. Many experts assumed it must be a hoax, but carbon-dating of samples of the vellum on which it is written has dated the manuscript to the early fifteenth century, and it is thought to have originated in central Europe.

Linguists and codebreakers were soon racing to decode the mysterious language, but it defied translation. It is thought the manuscript originally belonged to magician and astrologer John Dee (1527–1608) and then passed into the ownership of Holy Roman Emperor Rudolph II (1552–1612) and thence disappeared from records until it turned up in 1912. Since 1969 the manuscript has been housed at Yale's Beinecke Library.

Recent research using computer programmes to analyse the text have suggested that there is indeed a linguistic structure, implying it is not invented gibberish. However, the true meaning of the text continues to fascinate and elude in equal measure.

THE OLDEST KNOWN
BOOKS IN THE WORLD

Some of the oldest surviving intact books* in the world are described below.

PASTORAL CARE OF ST GREGORY THE GREAT
The oldest book entirely in the English language, this translation of the Latin text of Pope Gregory I was given by King Alfred to the Bishop of Worcester in the late ninth century. It came to the Bodleian Library in Oxford in 1671 (MS. Hatton 20).
Estimated age: 1,120 years old

THE BOOK OF KELLS
This beautiful illuminated manuscript contains the four Gospels of the New Testament. It was produced by monks (possibly on the Scottish isle of Iona) in *c.* 800 AD. Perceived as one of the greatest treasures of Celtic art, it is on display at Trinity Library, Dublin.
Estimated age: 1,216 years old

ST CUTHBERT GOSPEL
The St Cuthbert Gospel represents the oldest intact European book. It was buried with the body of St Cuthbert in Lindisfarne, Northumberland, in *c.* 698 BC and rediscovered in 1104 when the coffin was opened after it was moved to Durham Cathedral in 1104 to escape Viking raids. The beautiful embossed leather book was acquired

---

* Here a book is defined as a codex, made from folded leaves of paper.

by the British Library in 2012.
Estimated age: 1,318 years old

THE LEIDEN HERBARIA   A sixth-century copy of the fourth-century *Pseudo-Apuleius* herbarium – one of the most widely used herbaria of the medieval period – survives in Leiden University Library.
Estimated age: 1,466 years old

NAG HAMMADI LIBRARY   In 1945 a collection of Gnostic texts written in Coptic script were discovered by a farmer sealed in a jar in Nag Hammadi, Egypt. The leather-bound papyrus codices amounted to twelve volumes of religious texts, which were thought to have been written in the third and fourth centuries AD.
Estimated age: 1,700 years old

ETRUSCAN GOLD BOOK   The oldest known 'book'* in the world is made of pure gold and comprises just six pages, held together with gold rings. The book, discovered in an Etruscan tomb in western Bulgaria some sixty years ago, is thought to date back to 660 BC. The pages contain writing (in Etruscan, which is yet to be translated) and embossed with pictures of warriors, a lyre and a siren. The book was donated to Bulgaria's National History Museum in Sofia.
Estimated age: 2,675 years old

---

* Strictly speaking, although this gold object is shaped like a book, because it is created not from folded leaves but from separately crafted pages it cannot be truly described as a book.

A SHORT HISTORY OF THE COMIC

The telling of stories through pictures and words can be seen throughout history (some posit that early forerunners of comics include cave paintings or the Bayeux Tapestry). It was the eighteenth-century caricaturists, such as William Hogarth, James Gillray and Thomas Rowlandson, who popularized satirical pictures. Swiss-based artist Rodolphe Töpffer (1799–1846) was the first to create a comic strip: his poor eyesight led him to doodle rather than craft lifelike drawings to tell a story. Töpffer's *Histoire de M. Jabot* (1831) was his first published comic book, but it was *Histoire de M. Vieux Bois* (1837) (or *The Adventures of Obadiah Oldbuck* (1842) in America) that had a huge influence on the development of the genre.

In Britain the exciting yet trashy horror stories of the penny dreadful laid the foundation for serial stories. This was taken up by the humorous magazines such as *Judy*, which launched in 1867 and included a comic strip featuring Ally Sloper, a precursor of the 'naughty child' trope later seen in Dennis the Menace. Comics in Britain were mostly aimed at children but maintained a slightly subversive style. In 1921 the first D.C. Thomson title, *Adventure*, was launched, full of heroes and derring-do, and in 1929 in France the first Tintin comic strip appeared.

In America the first recognizably modern comic strip was Richard Felton Outcault's The Yellow Kid, which first appeared in 1895 in *The New York World*.

Early comic strips were found in popular newspapers and were intended to be funny (hence the name), but it was the creation of Superman by Jerome Siegal and Joseph Shuster in 1938 that really changed the genre and moved the idea of a comic book from an amusing short to a superhero-driven adventure. During the Second World War superhero comic books boomed as the public found solace and inspiration in the patriotic characters, such as Captain America. Today American superhero comics and British children's comics such as *The Beano* are still hugely popular, retaining and reflecting their influence on popular culture.

THE MOST POPULAR CHILDREN'S BOOKS

Below is a list of the some of the most beloved children's books and the dizzying number of copies they have estimated to have sold worldwide:

BOOK	COPIES
The Secret Diary of Adrian Mole, aged 13¾ (1982) by Sue Townsend	20 million
The Hunger Games (2008) by Suzanne Collins	23 million
The Wind in the Willows (1908) by Kenneth Grahame	25 million

The Very Hungry Caterpillar (1969) by Eric Carle	30 million
The Adventures of Pinocchio (1881) by Carlo Collodi	35 million
The Tale of Peter Rabbit (1902) by Beatrix Potter	45 million
Charlotte's Web (1952) by E.B. White	50 million
Watership Down (1972) by Richard Adams	50 million
Black Beauty (1877) by Anna Sewell	50 million
Anne of Green Gables (1908) by L.M. Montgomery	50 million
The Lion, the Witch and the Wardrobe (1950) by C.S. Lewis	85 million
Harry Potter and the Philosopher's Stone (1997) by J.K. Rowling*	107 million
The Little Prince (1943) by Antoine de Saint-Exupéry	140 million
The Hobbit (1947) by J.R.R. Tolkien	142 million

---

* I have not included in this list the other six Harry Potter books: each has sold over 50 million copies.

A SHORT HISTORY OF
DIGITAL PUBLISHING

Debate has raged over when the very first electronic book was published, in part because most new technologies take a while to be properly defined. But if we class an e-book as a work published in digital form, then early adopters would include Project Gutenberg, the first digital library, which since 1971 has been digitizing out-of-copyright documents and books of cultural importance, making them available online under open access. Equally, many reference works have been available on CD-ROM for a number of years – for example, the Oxford English Dictionary since 1989.

In 1987 Judith Malloy programmed and wrote a hypertext novel, *Uncle Roger*, which gave different narrative options depending on which link the reader chose: this was one of the first original fiction e-books. One of the first full novels to be published digitally was a thriller, *Host*, by Peter James, which came out on two floppy discs in 1993. But e-books did not really start to become mainstream until after 2000 when Stephen King released a novella, *Riding the Bullet*, the first mass-market e-book. It sold 500,000 copies in just forty-eight hours. Since then the market has steadily grown, especially in America, where by 2011 e-books were outselling traditional book formats on Amazon.

FONTS: SERIF AND SANS SERIF

Early fonts (*see page 37*) all contained serifs, the small flicks at the end of each letter as if written by a pen or with a brush stroke. It is thought serifs originated in Roman inscriptions carved onto stone; it is the serif that adds ornamentation to the lettering. A modern widely used serif font is:

Times New Roman

Serif fonts are considered much easier to read on the page than sans serif fonts, partly because the serifs at the bottom of the letters help create a stronger line for the eye to follow. Because of this serif fonts are generally used for the body of a book.

In the late nineteenth century, typeface designers introduced the sans serif fonts – *sans* meaning 'without' in French. William Caslon IV was one of the first designers to create a sans serif type, in 1816, but it took a while to catch on. By the 1920s, many more sans serif fonts had been developed and they became a popular font style for use in headings, titles, adverts and headlines. One of the most ubiquitous sans serif fonts is:

Helvetica

Helvetica was developed in 1957 by Swiss designer Max Miedinger. It is a clean, crisp font which lends itself extremely well to titles, company names and headlines.

Traditionally in book publishing serif fonts are used. Probably the most commonly used serif font is:

Garamond

However, as more and more people are taking to reading on a computer screen, sans serif fonts are becoming more popular for online content, so fonts such as **Futura** and Myriad are becoming more popular for use in e-books.

A SHORT HISTORY OF THE DICTIONARY

A dictionary is a collection of words (often ordered alphabetically) of one language with their meaning in the same or another language. A dictionary entry might include meaning, etymology, notes on pronunciation and usage. The earliest known dictionaries were discovered in modern-day Syria and were from the Akkadian Empire. They were written on cuneiform tablets in *c.* 2300 BC, and featured words from the Akkadian language translated into Sumerian. Many other early dictionaries exist from China, Japan, Greece and the Middle East.

In the medieval period dictionaries were more like a glossary, containing long lists of Latin words with alternatives in the vernacular. One of the earliest English-language dictionaries was Robert Mulcaster's *Elementarie*, published in 1582 and intended to promote the English language, which at that time was seen as the poor cousin of the more widely used Latin. It contained some 8,000 words in non-alphabetical order and without definitions; so although we recognize today many of the words used therein, such as 'elephant' and 'glitter', there are a number of words whose meanings have been lost, such as 'flindermouse'.

One of the first English-language dictionaries to include definitions was Thomas Blount's *Glossographia*, published in 1656. In 1755 Samuel Johnson's dictionary-defining tome *A Dictionary of the English Language* was published. Johnson's work was so thorough that it was recognized as a reliable source for English usage and set the tone for all future dictionaries. Entries were listed alphabetically and included definitions and quotations showing the word in context. It took Johnson and six assistants just eight years to compile the 40,000-word dictionary.

In 1879 Oxford University Press was asked to create a comprehensive English-language dictionary which would include historical, outmoded and lost words plus the most recent neologisms. The dictionary's editor, James Murray, was tireless in his search for words to include, and hundreds of volunteers joined in, searching old books and documents for words or quotations for consideration. These were passed to Murray as paper quotation slips, which he sifted through in his scriptorium. One of Murray's most avid contributors was an American Civil War veteran, Dr William Chester Minor, who was serving a life sentence in Broadmoor Asylum for shooting a man and consequentially had a lot of time on his hands. The full Oxford English Dictionary (OED) was finally published in 1928 and ran to twelve volumes, representing the most comprehensive guide to the English language. The OED is constantly updated by lexicographers and today contains over 600,000 words. Due to the popularity of the OED Online, the full OED is unlikely to be physically published again, however the single-volume Oxford Dictionary of English will continue to be reprinted.

NOVELS WITH MADE-UP LANGUAGES

A Clockwork Orange by Anthony Burgess (1962) Burgess, a keen linguist, invented a Russian-influenced argot called NADSAT for his teenage subclass to speak. The word Nadsat itself derives from the Russian word used as a suffix for the numbers 11–19, effectively making it a synonym for the English word 'teen'. Some examples of Nadsat: *droog* = friend; *pony* = to understand; *veck* = person.

Nineteen Eighty-four by George Orwell (1949) Orwell's dystopian novel introduces a new form of the English language, NEWSPEAK. Newspeak is intended to rid the language of superfluous words, eliminating synonyms and antonyms, leaving a staccato, uncluttered language which supposedly removes the need for thought and highlights the dominance of the state. Some examples of Newspeak: *Duckspeak* = to speak without thinking; *thoughtcrime* = to have dangerous or subversive thoughts; *unperson* = someone who has had all traces of themselves erased as if they never existed.

The Lord of the Rings by J.R.R. Tolkien (1955)   Tolkien invented two languages complete with their own alphabets for his epic novel. ELVISH (for which Tolkien created two versions, QUENYA and SINDARIN) is heavily influenced by Welsh and Finnish languages and has a musical, mystical character. Tolkien also alluded to several other invented languages in his books. Black Speech was invented by Sauron and used by the inhabitants of Mordor; it is in this language that the inscription on the One Ring is written. Some examples of Elvish: *alda* = tree; *duin* = river; *minas* = tower.

Watership Down by Richard Adams (1972)   Adams created a mythical language called LAPINE, which is spoken by the rabbits in his novels *Watership Down* and *Tales from Watership Down*. The language was never fully developed; Adams coined words as he went along, with the aim of creating a 'fluffy'-sounding language, suitable for rabbits. Some examples: *Homba* = a fox; *hrududu* = motor vehicle; *frith* = the sun.

A Song of Ice and Fire by George R.R. Martin   Martin created a language for the Dothraki, the nomadic horse-herding people. In his books Martin employed just a handful of words in DOTHRAKI, but in the television adaptation, *Game of Thrones*, the language has been much more fully developed. Some examples: *Qoy Qoyi* = blood of my blood; *khal* = warlord; *Me nem nesa* = it is known.

FAMOUS LAST LINES

A poignant or powerful closing line can stay with the reader. Bringing a novel to a satisfactory close is a great skill. The following novels have especially memorable last lines:

'So we beat on, boats against the current,
borne back ceaselessly into the past.'
The Great Gatsby (1925) by F. Scott Fitzgerald

'Oh, my girls, however long you may live, I never
can wish you a greater happiness than this.'
Little Women (1868) by Louisa May Alcott

'The offing was barred by a black bank of clouds, and
the tranquil waterway leading to the uttermost ends
of the earth flowed sombre under an overcast sky –
seemed to lead into the heart of an immense darkness.'
Heart of Darkness (1899) by Joseph Conrad

'Then starting home, he walked toward the trees,
and under them, leaving behind him the big sky, the
whisper of wind voices in the wind-bent wheat.'
In Cold Blood (1965) by Truman Capote

'At that, as if it had been the signal he waited for, Newland Archer got up slowly and walked back alone to his hotel.'
The Age of Innocence (1920) by Edith Wharton

'He turned out the light and went into Jem's room. He would be there all night, and he would be there when Jem waked up in the morning.'
To Kill a Mockingbird (1960) by Harper Lee

'But wherever they go, and whatever happens to them on the way, in that enchanted place on the top of the Forest a little boy and his Bear will always be playing.'
The House at Pooh Corner (1928) by A.A. Milne

'Yes, she thought, laying down her brush in extreme fatigue, I have had my vision.'
To the Lighthouse (1927) by Virginia Woolf

'And the ashes blew towards us with the salt wind from the sea.'
Rebecca (1938) by Daphne du Maurier

'I lingered round them, under that benign sky; watched the moths fluttering among the heath, and hare-bells; listened to the soft wind breathing through the grass; and wondered how anyone could ever imagine unquiet slumbers, for the sleepers in that quiet earth.'
Wuthering Heights (1847) by Emily Brontë

'After all, tomorrow is another day.'
Gone with the Wind (1936) by Margaret Mitchell

TIMELINE OF THE
DEVELOPMENT OF THE BOOK

The earliest manuscripts were written on scrolls – long pieces of parchment or papyrus on which the text was written in columns and the work rolled into a scroll. These manuscripts may have had rollers at either end to make unrolling the scroll easier, allowing the reader to read by unrolling one side while rolling up the other. In India in the first century the first 'books' appeared. These were religious works written on flat palm leaves in lampblack (*see page 73*) and then held flat by sewing them between two wooden boards. From the second century AD codices began to creep into use. A codex is the early form of a modern book, with pages and a cover. It is much more economical with parchment than a scroll, as both sides of the page can be written upon and it can be transported and shelved more easily, perhaps in part explaining why the codex soon became the favoured shape for books in the Western world. See below for a timeline of the development of the book:

2400 BC	Earliest surviving papyrus scrolls produced in Egypt
c.600 BC	Writing in Europe became more standardized, proceeding from left to right
500–400 BC	Parchment made from animal skins used as an alternative to papyrus in Greece

400–300 BC	Writing on silk introduced in China
c.295 BC	The Library at Alexandria founded
c.200 BC	Wax tablets developed by the Romans and Greeks
150 BC–40 AD	Creation of the Dead Sea Scrolls in Hebrew and Aramaic
c.150 AD	Paper made from vegetable fibres developed in China
150–450	Gradual move away from scrolls and towards codex book form
610	Papermaking technology introduced to Japan from China
868	The *Diamond Sutra*, the oldest example of a woodblock printed book, created in China
895	Oldest surviving use of a colophon in *Books of the Prophets* by Moses ben Asher in Israel
c. 1000	Papermaking technology reached Moorish Spain
c. 1041–48	The first moveable type developed in China
1200–1300	In Italy book production moved from monastic scriptoria to secular scribes in major cities
c. 1230	Metal moveable type developed in Korea
1255	Paper mill established in Genoa
1338	The oldest known paper mill established in France

1403	Stationers' Company founded in London
1423	Oldest surviving example of woodblock printing in Europe, a picture of St Christopher, was produced; it is held at the John Rylands Library, Manchester
1439–50	Johannes Gutenberg developed metal moveable type
1455	Gutenberg printed the *Gutenberg Bible*, the first book in Europe to be printed with moveable type
1457	The Mainz Psalter printed by Johann Fust and Peter Schoeffer, the first book to be printed in more than one colour
1476	William Caxton established a press in Westminster
1495	The first English paper mill established by John Tate in Hertfordshire
1501	Aldus Manutius invented italic type and the octavo book format in Venice
1534	Cambridge University Press established; printed its first book in 1583
1605	First newspaper, *Relation aller Fürnemmen und gedenckwürdigen Historien*, printed in Strasbourg
1621	*The Corante*, the first English newspaper, was printed
1640	The *Bay Psalm Book*, the first book to be printed in North America
1709	Statute of Anne passed in England, the first copyright law in the world

1755	Samuel Johnson's *A Dictionary of the English Language* published
1796	Lithographic printing invented by Alois Senefelder
1798	William Stanhope invented the iron-cast press, replacing the wooden printing press
1812	Friedrich Koenig invented the steam-powered cylinder press
1832–60	The rise of the penny dreadful and other cheap books aimed at the masses
1840s	Wood was used to make pulp for paper in Germany
1886	Berne Convention established international copyright reciprocity
1886	Linotype printing press invented, revolutionizing typesetting
1935	The first Penguin paperbacks published
1995	Amazon, the first online bookseller launched
2000	*Riding the Bullet* by Stephen King became the first mass-market electronic book
2004	Sony Librie, the first dedicated e-book reader, was released

INDEX

academic books, most
    influential 62–3
Amazon 13–14, 117, 128
Apostles society 86
Austen, Jane 17, 25, 33,
    46, 92
authors
    families 31–2
    juvenilia 91–2
    most prolific 39–40
    most translated 14
    noms de plume 3–4
    oldest debut 106–7
    quotations on books
        93–4
    writing tips 16, 105–6
    youngest debut 36

Baileys Women's Prize for
    Fiction 60–61

Bay Psalm Book 35
Bible, making of 42–3
Bloomsbury Group 64–5
Bodleian Libraries 53, 96
book and manuscript terms
    75–9
book fairs *see* Frankfurt
Book of the Dead 7
book(s)
    banned 9–13
    bestselling of all time
        45
    capitals 8
    development, timeline
        125–8
    first editions 58–9
    first English printed 27
    lost 82–5
    mistakes in printing
        99–101

most translated 104–5
oldest known 112–13
paper 63–4
prizes and awards
    60–61, 68–9, 98–9
series, naming 5–6
signed 49
sizes, traditional
    109–10
superlatives 43–5
terms 75–9
titles, oddest 70
towns 72–3
bookbinding 107–9
bookplates 96–7
bookshop
    oldest in the world 55
    world's largest 97
British Library 96, 108
Brontë, Charlotte 4, 31, 91

Cambridge University
    Press 57–8
Camus, Albert 30, 34, 69
Capote, Truman 34, 123
Carroll, Lewis 3
Caxton, William 27, 127
chapbooks 65–6
Chekhov, Anton 4
children's books, most
    popular 115–16
Christie, Agatha 4, 14, 17,
    48, 50, 55, 56
comics, history of 114–15

copyright 28, 71
Costa Prize 61

detection club, the 50
Dickens, Charles 29, 32,
    45, 46, 93, 97
dictionary, short history of
    119–21
digital publishing, history
    of 117
dust jackets 87–8

Eliot, George 4, 47, 106
Ellis, Bret Easton 22–3, 36

first editions, identifying
    58–9
Fitzgerald, F. Scott 30, 34,
    88, 123
fonts 37–9, 118–19
Frankfurt Book Fair
    19–20

Gaskell, Elizabeth 33
glossary of book and
    manuscript terms 75–9
Gutenberg Bible 44–5
Gutenberg, Johannes 15,
    37, 74, 80–81, 127

Hardy, Thomas 85
Hemingway, Ernest 47,
    56, 69, 83, 93, 100
Homer 82–3

illuminated manuscripts 88–91
incunabula 15, 77
ink 73–5
ISBN numbers 51–2

Joyce, James 12, 54, 83
juvenilia 91–2

Kafka, Franz 30, 34, 94
King, Stephen 3, 14, 21–2, 39, 117, 128

Lane, Allen 55–7
languages, made-up 121–2
legal deposit 95–6
Lessing, Doris 30, 69, 107
libraries 7–8, 18, 19, 53, 87, 91–3, 95–6, 108, 111, 112–13
literary families 31–2
literary movements of note 29–30

Man Booker Prize 60
Mills & Boon 67–8
Mitchell, David 21
Mitchell, Margaret 54, 60, 124
movies that started life as books 24–6
Murakami, Haruki 22

Nabokov, Vladimir 33

Neruda, Pablo 4
Nobel Prize in Literature 68–9
noms de plume 3–4
novels
    continuation 16–17
    famous last lines 123–4
    famous opening lines 46–7
    recurring characters 21–3
    sequences 5–6
    titles, alternative 48
    unfinished 32–3

oldest debut novelists 106–7
oldest known books 112–13
Orwell, George 2, 4, 16, 46, 62, 121

paper, history of 101–3
papyrus 7–8
Penguin paperbacks 55–7
poets laureate 98–9
Potter, Beatrix 53
publishing house, oldest 57–8
publishing rejections 53–4
Pulitzer Prize 60

quills 41
quotations on books and reading 93–4

Rowling, J.K. 4, 5, 6, 48, 54, 100, 116
Ruskin, John 93

Samuel Johnson Prize 61
scriptoria 18
Shakespeare, William 14, 45, 62, 82, 103
signed books 49
Stationers' Company 52–3
Stevenson, Robert Louis 92

Tennyson, Alfred, Lord 92, 98, 86
timeline, development of the book 125–8
Tolkien, J.R.R. 5, 116, 122
translated authors, most 14
translated books, most 104–5

Twain, Mark 3, 33, 100
typefaces *see* fonts

UNESCO World Book Capitals 8

vellum 23–4, 42, 80
Voltaire 4, 9
Vonnegut, Kurt 22, 30, 105
Voynich Manuscript 111

Woolf, Virginia 30, 65, 124
World Book Day 103–4
writers, most prolific 39–40
writing tips
    George Orwell's 16
    Kurt Vonnegut's 105–6

youngest debut writers 36